Moving the Troops

(Ten Years of Living in a Muslim Village)

By
Donald Raun

Moving the Troops

Permission has been granted by Inter Varsity Press to use several quotations from the following books by Eugene H. Peterson: *Run with the Horses* and *A Long Obedience in the Same Direction.*

Photo on cover: Dugout conoes on the Chari River in Chad. (By author)

Printed by Faith & Fellowship Press
1020 W. Alcott Ave., Fergus Falls, MN 56537

ISBN: 0-943167-58-2

Contents

Preface

Three years ago, *Christianity Today* reported that only six percent of missionaries in the world at that time were focused on reaching Muslims. Now, perhaps a percentage point more. Orpha and I were privileged to be among that category of missionaries for our last ten years in Chad. This book chronicles some of our experiences of those years. The title, *Moving the Troops,* is taken from an American Civil War story which the reader will find in chapter 5. Often, we felt we were less than adequate for the task before us, but, by God's inscrutable will, we found ourselves among the "troops" that helped bring God's message to Muslims. We were moved by God's compassion for these people who have so seldom known personally any follower of Christ.

Another book, *Who Would Have Thought...!,* tells the story of our family in Africa, covering the four decades between 1959 and 1999. We were a missionary family with very ordinary gifts and talents, and Orpha and I often made the remark to each other, as we were surprised at God's grace working through us, "Who Would Have Thought!" Who would have thought that we would ever get involved in Bible translation... or teaching classes on the Christian Family...or writing Bible study books and other literature...or living in a Muslim village for ten years...or, finally, sticking it out for 40 years? It's been one big adventure of watching God work!

—Donald Raun

"I will go before you and will level the mountains;
I will break down gates of bronze
and cut through bars of iron."
Isaiah 45:2

1
The Man in the White Gown

The day began like any other day. I had an errand that morning in the administrative part of town. While there, a stranger who worked in the immigration office stopped me. Could he get a ride with me back to the residential part of town? "Sure, no problem." As we drove, he asked me another question. Would I be willing to teach him English? His work in the immigration office brought him into contact from time to time with people who knew only English – especially with those coming from Nigeria.

As missionaries involved mostly in teaching and translating the Bible during the almost 30 years we had then spent in Chad, we did not feel that teaching English to anybody should be a priority. Somehow, though, I could not turn down Ali Bah's request. I told him I would see what I could do. And I invited him to come over to our house when he had the time.

Dressed in an immaculate white gown, Ali Bah came over one day. As he came to our front door, Orpha was coming out our back door with a pail of dirty water. She greeted him while she threw the water on some flower plants. His quizzical look prompted her to explain: "We recycle all the water we use because we have no well." Ali Bah did not offer his hand for the normal handshake that a friendly encounter in Africa usually demands. Which surprised Orpha and prompted an explanation on his part: "I never shake hands with women." Any suspicion of unfriendliness, though, was dissipated when Ali Bah next showed his concern over our not having a well. Then Orpha excused herself for a moment and rang a bell to summon me at my study in the book warehouse down a path. Noting that Ali Bah had come, I hurried to the house. After chatting together a bit, we made arrangements to start English classes for him and for two other men who had also shown an interest in learning English. After our "au revoirs", Orpha and I commented on Ali Bah's friendliness and decency.

The tribe from which Ali Bah came would win no popularity contest in southern Chad. The Bagirmi people used to be those who raided villages for slaves. For centuries they made their livelihood by swooping down on the heavily populated villages of that part of Chad, often traveling up the wide Chari River (pronounced Shah-Ree) in their large canoes, snatching people to sell to the Arab slave-traders who operated further north. Slave-raiders and slave-traders, working together. Thousands of innocent people killed, thousands of homes broken up mercilessly through the centuries. The southern Chadians have hated and feared the Bagirmi people for a long, long time. But Ali Bah didn't impress us as one to avoid. He was the first Bagirmi person we had ever met as far as we knew and we liked him from the start.

Three times a week Ali Bah would come to our house. When I felt I could no longer spend so much time teaching English, Orpha took over. And when, after a time, the other two men dropped out of the classes, Ali Bah persisted. My time with him became limited to accompanying him, in polite African fashion, a distance back to his home after each class period. On these walks, I learned about him and his people and their religion. They had been Muslims for over 450 years – since the days of Martin Luther!

Orpha developed into an enthusiastic and skillful teacher of English. As Ali Bah's knowledge grew, she began using rather innovative teaching methods and they obviously worked well on him. One method she used extensively was composing simple crossword puzzles which were based on interesting stories from the Good News version of the Bible. She would type out the passage for each puzzle from this simple translation which he would read and then search for the answers in that passage. He loved this! And two things were happening at the same time: Ali Bah was becoming Bible-literate and Ali Bah was learning English!

During those three years that he came regularly to our house, Ali Bah remained a devout Muslim. He was observing things about us. One time Orpha had bread baking in the oven as she was tutoring Ali Bah and his two companions and our son David had just come into the house. She asked him, "David, would you please take the bread out of the oven?" Ali Bah turned to his friends and remarked, "They don't use the imperative (don't command) in this house!" Courtesy between family members was something that impressed him, evidently. He noticed, too, that our missionary friends who passed through from time to time lived and worked among various tribal peoples, learning their languages as they did. One day while discussing the plight of his people who had no written language and thus no books nor any means of writing letters to their own people in their language, he remarked to us that only missions put people's languages into writing.

Was God beginning to tell us something through Ali Bah? Was He using this devout Muslim to call us into a ministry among the unpopular Bagirmi Muslims? More and more it seemed that God was doing just that! I doubt that Ali Bah ever had in mind that we should some day live and work among his people, but we were becoming more open to the idea.

The local Christians began noticing that we were spending a lot of time with a certain man with a long gown and a Muslim cap. Their women noticed when Orpha greeted Ali Bah's wife in the market-place. Why, she was even using the Muslim woman's language! The Mundang Christians didn't like what they saw and heard.

The word got around eventually that we were considering moving away from Lere to live among those "fierce Bagirmi people", as the president of our synodical church body (who was a Mundang) called them. When I later officially announced our desire to work among the Bagirmi to both the church in Africa and our mission board in the homeland, we had a difficult time persuading them that God was really calling us out of the Mundang area and calling us to a far-away all-Muslim tribe. We were in our mid-fifties and perhaps the thought occurred to some that we were going through a mid-life crisis! And we ourselves had a few questions: 1.) How does one bring God's message to Muslims? 2.) Would they accept us to live and work among them? 3.) Could we learn another language? And there were more!

2
The End of an Era

While we were still working among the Mundang people in the mid-1980s, I was challenged one day by a Mundang pastor to rethink our priorities. I was teaching a course on Church and Mission History at our seminary in Cameroon at the time. "We don't often see missionaries going out these days to evangelize people who don't know Christ. You people are involved in many other things, but you don't evangelize." That's the gist of his words as I remember them. I had been teaching future pastors the importance of having evangelistic vision if we are to have a strong church. What about myself? Would I be willing to bring the Gospel into new and inhospitable areas where it is not known? I had something to think about!

A missionary from another mission was beginning to work among Muslims in central Cameroon about the time that God began speaking to us to consider entering a new era in our lives. He wrote in a church paper: "Jesus said to Simon (in Luke 5:4),

Canoe market at Mesken

5

'Push the boat out further to the deep water and you and your partners let down your nets for a catch.' Peter was probably thinking, 'Lord, we never go fishing there because one can't expect to catch fish in such deep water.' But you know the outcome of the story. Up until these recent years, we too have not gone fishing in these deep waters....We have been peering into those waters and inspecting our nets. Let us let them down; the results are in the Lord's hands."

For missionaries, too, it is not easy to leave what seems to offer security and success and head into uncharted waters. Several books by Eugene H. Peterson, the author of *The Message* version of the Bible, were often at my side during the days leading up to our leaving Lere to live among the Bagirmi people. One of those was on the life of the prophet Jeremiah and called, *Run with the Horses*. A couple quotes from that book: "He (Jeremiah) worked seriously and imaginatively to show the people that they were not the only people that God had dealings with, and that the life of faith necessarily involves us in a worldwide community that includes strange-appearing, strange-acting and strange-sounding people. Biblical faith always has and always will have this global dimension to it." Later in the book he quotes the great missionary statesman of a century ago, John R. Mott: "The missionary activities of the church are the circulation of its blood, which would lose its vital power if it never flowed to the extremities." Peterson challenged me in this book to trust God to carry out His purpose which was to get the Good News to all corners of the globe. Even using us to go to some obscure village in Chad? Even though we were middle-aged missionaries, considered by many too old to try new paths?

Other books by Peterson helped us. One day we ran across some helpful comments on Psalm 107:16 in his book, *A Year with the Psalms*. That verse spoke to me: "For he breaks down gates of bronze and cuts through bars of iron." To us the citadel of Islam seemed at times to be utterly impenetrable. But even that could tumble before God's superior power! I began believing that, until it became a strong conviction. Another book of Peterson's titled *Traveling Light* (a commentary on the Letter to the Galatians) reminded me that it is God's will to deliver us from this present evil age – not to remove us from dangerous places and situations but to rescue us from the evil powers of this age. So we could trust Him to carry us through the dangers ahead! And God's message could bring freedom even to the Muslims. They could travel light! In his book, *A Long Obedience in the Same Direction* on Psalms 120 – 135, I read that God "stuck with them (the Hebrew Christians) so consistently and surely that they learned how to stick with God." So they could run with perseverance the race that was set before them. (Hebrews 12:1-2) We needed to learn "stick-to-it-iveness." And it helps immensely to know, as Peterson's comments on Psalm 129 indicate, that "God sticks to his relationship. He establishes a personal relationship with us and stays with us." I was beginning to realize more that Muslims didn't know anything about a personal and intimate relationship with God. We wanted to be at God's disposal so that we could somehow bring the message to Muslims that God very much wants to establish such a relationship with them. But to be at God's disposal seemed more and more to mean that we would be "bumping into" Bagirmi Muslims, of which Ali Bah could be only the first of many! An era of ministry primarily aimed at discipling Christians was ending for us. Almost 30 years of reaping what others had sown; now it began looking like sowing time in a new field might be around the corner. We were thankful for the people and books that God brought to our attention to encourage us in the new venture.

3
The Angel on the Highway

How many people have seen angels? We have our own ideas of how angels should look and maybe we wouldn't recognize an angel if we saw one! Mostly, they are invisible messengers of God, sent to do his bidding – to protect us in times of danger, to guide us, to help us in all sorts of ways. At other times God chooses to use quite ordinary-looking folk to do the same tasks. The end results can be the same.

I was driving alone down a highway in Chad one day. I had left off our son Jonathan at N'Djamena and was now returning home. But I had much more on my mind than merely driving home. I took a different route than I usually took, hoping to run into Bagirmi people who were supposed to live in the general area through which I was driving. I prayed for guidance as I drove. I had passed one village after another, but none of them had seemed to me to be a Bagirmi village. Not that I knew exactly what a Bagirmi village should look like. I had, however, lived long enough in Africa to recognize some tribes by the way they built their houses and granaries, by the ladders they used, by the animals they kept, whether their homes were built close together or far from their neighbors, and so on. Some villages through which I had passed looked like Arab villages; some looked like Massa villages.

One village large enough to merit a name sign by the side of the road caught my attention. The name on the sign-post, Mai Lao, made me think I was driving in Vietnam! I stopped in the middle of the village and a stranger quickly walked up to me. "Can I help you?" he asked in passable French. I told him I was driving through on my way home to Lere and I wanted to know if any Bagirmi people lived in the area. I told him I had a Bagirmi friend in my home village and would like to meet more of them. "I am a Bagirmi myself and if you want to take me with you in your car, I could introduce you right now to some of my people." I said, "Fine!" and off we went.

Saleh Moda, my new guide, took me first to see the chief of the Bagirmi sector of Mai Lao. Being a large village, several tribes lived within its confines and when we came to the Bagirmi neighborhood, I was excited to see some of Ali Bah's people. Then, when he was willing to go with me to other villages, I was even more so.

As we drove along through Bagirmi-Land, Saleh told me about his people and a little about the villages in the area. We

Chief Hassan, David and Idi

finally came to a small village on the banks of the Chari (Shah-Ree) River. We stopped at an imposing cluster of mud-walled buildings near the edge of the village. The chief was home, seated on a mat with several men around him. The fact that they were there and not out in their fields was surprising, given the time of the day and the season. Blama (chief) Hassan listened intently as Saleh introduced me to him. Talking in their own language, I don't know what they said between themselves but it was obvious that the chief was interested in me and he invited me to come back to his village another time. The chief knew Ali Bah's mother-in-law who lived only a couple miles away in another

9

village, and hearing that I was a friend of Ali Bah must have helped to authenticate my story and make me more acceptable. I took Saleh Moda back to Mai Lao where the chief of the Bagirmi sector invited me to stay overnight in his home. I remember how intent he was that evening, as we sat under the stars, on teaching me some Bagirmi, going through the numbers 1 through 10 with me many times until I could say them to his satisfaction. That was quite a day and I won't ever forget it!

A couple months later I returned to the small all-Muslim village of Mesken where I had been so well received by its chief. This time I stayed several days at the chief's home. It was the rainy season and most of the village population were in the fields. Left largely to myself during the working hours, I had lots of time to roam around the area and explore. What interesting things to see! The dugout canoes transporting people to and from fields across the river. The hawk-eyed river birds swooping swiftly to grab their prey in its waters. The huge banyan trees with their wide-spreading branches held up by runners descending from those branches to root themselves in the soil below. A nearby orchard of mango trees sitting on a bluff above the river. On the same property, maintained by a high-ranking government official living in N'Djamena, were other tropical trees such as stately royal palms and large grotesque baobabs, planted long ago by some French colonial who wanted a place to retreat from his labors in the hot capital. I also explored a scenic path along a small river connecting the two large rivers, the Chari and the Logone, the latter running parallel to the Chari and forming the boundary of Cameroon some 20 miles away. The water in this small connecting river, called the Loumia, could flow either way depending on which of the two big rivers had the higher water level at any time.

Jande was one of the few in the village who knew a little French. He was about twelve and attended a nearby public school that taught in the French language. But the Muslims largely ignored the school. Their leaders in Chad had long felt that learning the French language was to take on the decadent ways of the West and people in Mesken wanted to keep in step with their fellow Muslims. So they kept their children at home.

However, Jande was from one of the more progressive families in the area and he was permitted to attend "the white man's school." And so I had someone to help me learn a little basic Bagirmi those days – when he wasn't doing something else. We would sit on a big log in a conspicuous place in the village. He would tell me the Bagirmi equivalents of the things we saw around us or the activities of the people passing by. For instance, if a child passed by crying, I might ask Jande how one would say, "This child is crying." Then, "This child is not crying." Or, "This child cried yesterday." Then, I would substitute "woman" and "man" or "boy" and "girl" for "child" and then other action words to replace "crying." I could find out many things about the language just from a few simple sentences such as these. I would write each sentence down, using a phonetic alphabet learned in a linguistic course 30 years earlier. This way I could pronounce each utterance back to Jande in a fairly understandable fashion. Later, I would practice by myself.

Blama Hassan must have decided that I liked his people. At any rate, he invited me after my stay of several days to return later. But not alone next time. "Bring your family and you can live in one of my houses until you can build one of your own," he said before I left his village.

What if Saleh Moda had not been with me that day I was looking for Bagirmi people? I probably would never have found Mesken or if I did I would not have been welcomed as I was. A white stranger just doesn't walk into a small Muslim village and get a warm reception without someone along to pave the way for him. God had had His eye on Mesken village for a long time and He provided me with a person who came to my aid for that all-important initial visit. You may call Saleh Moda, whom we never saw again, an angel if you wish. We do.

4
Two Women on the Highway

"Having a worthy goal is what truly matters," wrote an Englishwoman recalling her early days in East Africa. She started her life in Africa as a cripple in her early twenties and she knew from the start that her life in the rugged tropics would not be easy. But she was determined to overcome all difficulties because she had a worthy goal.

After my first visit to Mesken I had a strong feeling that we might live there some day. Orpha, too, felt that way though she had never seen the place. But what was our goal when we began thinking of moving to a small Muslim village where we would be the only whites and the only Christians? Simply this: To so live and work among Muslims in a village setting that they would one day be convinced of the truth of our message and accept our Savior as their own. How many years would that take and what would it involve on our part? We didn't have a clue, but we knew that God was calling us in this direction. Perhaps one could say that equally important to having a goal is to be confident of God's calling so that one can depend on His continual support. If we aren't confident that God has called us to a difficult task, there will be discouragements, failures and setbacks from which we will never have the strength to recover.

We had time to ponder God's calling to go to Mesken before we finally picked up and left. A year and a half went by between my initial contact with Blama Hassan and the day we arrived as a family to live in his village. Those were some of the most difficult days of our lives.

As I was driving one day to N'Djamena, I saw a camel crossing the highway just ahead of me. It was no more used to such things as blacktop highways than I was used to seeing camels. It fell down in a most awkward-looking jumble of legs sprawled out in every direction! This animal was created for desert sand – not blacktop highways! But camels were moving down fron the north into situations never before encountered, as their owners searched for areas where there would be enough water and forage to keep their animals alive. I wrote in my journal on March 4, 1989, after noting this event and the adjustments that camels were having to make to live further south: "On the other hand, we are moving into the area further north and we, too, will have some adjusting to do!"

I had my moments of doubting whether we could, indeed, keep on the course. In a journal entry of several months before the above, I wrote: "These days I sense my great weakness as I contemplate a building operation and moving to Mesken." I had the scare of my life years ago as a teenager in Seattle when a friend and I set out to cross a seven-mile stretch of Puget Sound in a little fishing boat powered by no more than a 10-horse engine. Jack and I were dawdling along, watching Bainbridge Island loom larger straight ahead of us. Suddenly... "Hey," one of us yelled, "there's a freighter on the right coming straight for us!" Though a mile or two away from us then, it was indeed coming up very fast and silently, like a huge bull elephant coming at a hunter from his side. We were close to – or maybe past – the point of no return! A decision had to be made immediately: Keep going with the hope of beating the ship – or turn quickly around? We did the latter, but we didn't escape some huge waves made by the passing ship on its way to Elliot Bay. I don't remember the rest of that day, but I doubt very much if we thought any more about the island we were planning to explore! This and other scares in my life when I'd had to change course suddenly may have conditioned me to sense a little caution about our getting involved in a moving operation like we were now contemplating.

It's interesting and instructive to note that during those days when we were feeling inner turmoil over the uncertainties ahead, my journal entries are fuller with assurances of God's helping hand than at any other time in my life. After returning from that first stint of several days at Mesken in July, 1988, I came across a couple passages in the Bible that seemed to speak directly to me: "Do not be terrified, do not be afraid of them. The Lord your God, who is going before you, will fight for you, as he did for you in Egypt, before your very eyes, and in the desert. There you saw how the Lord your God carried you, as a father carries his son, all the way you went until you reached this place." (Deut. 1:29-31) The second passage in chapter 31 of the same book, verses 1-8, ends with these words: "The Lord himself goes before you and will be with you; he will never leave you nor forsake you. Do not be afraid; do not be discouraged." I felt then that just as the Israelites were on the verge of crossing the Jordan River to enter new and unmanageable situations, so were we poised to enter new territory in our lives. I noted that the writer of the Book of Hebrews wrote these same words for the needs of his readers centuries later (Hebrews 13:5); why then couldn't I apply them to our situation? After all, our Lord is "the same yesterday, today and forever."

Those days our son Jonathan was also experiencing new situations. God had called him many years previously to spend his life ministering to Muslims in northern Chad and now he was finally living among some of them in a small Arab village north of N'Djamena. On my way to Mesken that summer, we spent a couple of good days together there, contemplating the future. He told me he would be reaching two goals he had set for himself for his first year back in Africa after spending some years in America going to school and working. The goals: To harvest a crop he had raised himself, and to have gotten a good start in learning Arabic. That Sunday, which happened to be the day of the most important Muslim holiday (celebrating Abraham's willingness to offer up his son to God), we sat together in the middle of the peanut field he had planted on a small segment of the vast sun-washed plains north of the capital. We talked about the faithfulness of God in our lives. Nothing like the setting of a quiet peanut field for doing that! After a while, his new friend, Adida, came along, carrying some pieces of mutton that he wanted to share with us. We ate, and Jonathan and his friend chatted in Arabic while I listened. I could tell that our son was content and at ease. He had found his niche!

Would we find ours? Would we experience such content-ment ourselves? While at Mesken a few days later, I felt again and again that God had gone before and was preparing the way for us. One day I stood on the bank of the Chari River, looking across in a north-easterly direction. I could probably travel thousands of miles in that direction without coming across a single outpost of Christian believers! The wide river before me was pretty much the dividing point then between the Christian and Muslim sections of Chad. And stretching further on the other side were the vast Islamic areas of northern Sudan, the Arabian peninsula, Iran and Afghanistan. Beyond those, the millions of unreached people in the Central Asian republics, northwest China, Mongolia and Siberia. Why should the Christian world concentrate so much on reaching the more accessible areas west and south of the Chari while neglecting those east and north?

I studied Arabic with more determination after my first visit of several days in Mesken. I thought it would be handy to know some Arabic, at least, if we were to live in an Arabic-speaking area of Chad. I did other things. Fellow missionaries were told of our desire to leave the Mundang area and live in a Muslim village. Letters were written to the States and to the synodical office of our church in Africa. The hardest of all was informing the local people. I lost sleep over how to do that! After one particularly tough night I found a verse (Isaiah 8:13) that seemed to tell me I should fear no man, only God. That I should above all fear being disobedient to Him to the point that His Presence could no longer abide with me. Along with that verse, God seemed to give me a text and an outline of what I should say to the Mundang Christians. The text was in Isaiah, chapter 5; the outline included the thoughts that God had invested so much in the Mundang people, giving His Word to them so bountifully. They had the entire Bible! Now, others needed to get that same Word – the people that didn't have even a page of it in their language. Judgment descends on people who treat lightly what they have received from God. When I spoke these words to the local Christians a few days later, did they truly receive this message as God's? Some did, I believe, but not all.

I had a grand time when I visited the Mesken villagers again for several days at the end of October. One day I watched several men hollowing out two canoes. Two men would work together on one canoe, keeping their axes from hitting each other with great skill. I next watched a young man making a fish trap – a fascinating device! One day I recorded some children singing. Women in the chief's compound wanted me to play back the recording later that afternoon. They laughed and giggled while their ears listened and their hands cut pieces of gumbo. Every afternoon I watched boys play soccer on a broad expanse of sandy ground next to the river. Younger boys were all taken up with making what they called "paransits." Evidently they had recently seen some soldiers at the nearby military base parachute from a plane on some practice maneuvers. So the rage among these boys was to find plastic bags and old erasers (used for weights) and make these minature parachutes and throw them skyward. They vied with each other to see which "paransit" would float down the best. I thought they were quite creative!

I heard lots of Bagirmi being spoken those days. It was harvest time and people enjoyed getting together. The evenings were cozy at the chief's compound with many family members sitting around and talking. It was a good thing I had not taken my family with me, however, as the chief had suggested I do three months earlier. There had been a very hard rainy season that year and the building the chief had said we could use had tumbled down.

I received another strong confirmation that we were heading in the right direction. One day as I drove on a certain stretch of road, I saw a small Suzuki car heading my way. I slowed down and this car did, too. I saw the logo on its sides, that of WEC Mission. I stopped when I noticed they did and walked over to the car. Inside were two women and a man. They were British missionaries taking their mission director on a tour of the area. We chatted a bit and I told them about our interest in the Bagirmi people of Mesken and the possibility of living among these people. I discovered that these ladies had started working three or four years earlier in a Bagirmi village about a hundred miles south. They had been praying that God would send a missionary couple to help reach the Bagirmi people for Christ. They felt that it really took a man to witness to Muslim men and that if men became interested in the Gospel, then it would be possible to reach the women too. And then Pauline and Liz said something I shall never forget: "Perhaps you are the couple that we have been praying for!" I asked them how they felt about Lutheran missionaries being the answer to their prayers! "No problem," they said, "we can work together."

We later learned that others had also been praying for the Bagirmi people. When we went back to the States on leave a couple years later, we discovered that an old friend of ours from Seattle had prayed for the Bagirmi for several years before we became interested in them. Our mission had no plans for reaching them during those praying days, but she had seen this name, Bagirmi, listed among the unreached people groups in the world in an issue of the *Global Prayer Digest*, and she received a burden from God to start praying for them. Also, we made phone contact with the leader of a ladies' prayer group in Jackson, Tennessee, who, along with her friends, had been praying for the Bagirmi. The elderly lady couldn't remember where she first heard the name.

Two women on the highway... How much it meant to us at that time to get their encouragement! They recognized that we could be the ones whom God had chosen to be His instruments for answering the prayer that they constantly brought before God those days: "God, send a couple to work among the Bagirmi!" Knowing this, could we then possibly turn away from what God seemed to be leading us to do?

5
Moving the Troops

I read a story about Stonewall Jackson the year that we moved to Mesken. General Jackson was moving his troops through Virginia when his army found its progress blocked by a river. He ordered his engineers to take measures needed to get his artillery and wagons across. He also called for his wagon-master and told him to move the wagon train across the river without delay. The wagon-master started immediately to implement the order, working with anything at his disposal (rocks, fence rails, etc.). He quickly made a bridge of sorts and got the supplies across. The next morning he reported to Jackson: "The troops are all across the river the way you said." The engineers, however, were still in their tent, drawing pictures and designing their bridge.

I read this story in a book entitled, *Priority One: What God Wants*. It's author, Norm Lewis, makes an application following this story: "Our churches in our land have rivers to cross in order to send an army of witnesses to the 2.7 billion people who have never heard of Jesus Christ. Have we tackled that task? Are we even designing bridges?" The author's own father visited West Africa once as a 60-year-old businessman. He was grieved over the lack of dental care in that part of Africa. When he returned home, he enrolled in a school of dentistry; after finishing his studies he went back to Africa with a dental clinic. In his years there he met the dental needs of over 700 Christian workers. He later went to Latin America and the Orient, doing the same work. In all, he worked 15 years as a dentist around the world.

At the time I wrote these anecdotes in my journal I was not yet 60 years old, but close. I suppose I wrote them down because they inspired me. Maybe Orpha and I could yet manage to change direction in our lives – maybe we could get the Word of God across the river. By this time we were very eager to try.

The setting sun had cast a golden glow on the foliage of a huge tree under which a large number of Mundang church leaders sat. It was their annual 3-day conference in January, 1989. I wrote in my journal that I felt a certain sadness as I looked over the sea of black faces in front of me. Men that I had worked with – some of them for almost 30 years – had just heard my"farewell speech". Would I ever again address such a large group of Christian men? The sun had been setting while I spoke on the apostle Paul's words in Acts 20:32. As the sun set, so our work among the Mundang ended. I had told the men that although I could not say many of the things that Paul said in this chapter of Acts, I could commit them to God and to the Word which could build them up – the Word which they then held in their hands. Our hope was that this Word would also some day be in the hands of the Bagirmi Muslims, bringing light into their hopeless lives.

An instructor in the Prairie Bible Institute of Canada once told his class: "Don't be hopeless, just be helpless!" Orpha and I weren't hopeless like the Bagirmi people without Christ, but we did feel helpless in those days immediately preceding the building of our house in Mesken. Orpha has always been interested in drawing house plans and she got a chance to design our 30 by 15 foot dwelling. Because we had limited resources with which to work, our house was going to be small. Because it was going to be so small, it had to be designed carefully to ensure our earthly possessions would all fit in. I may have had a small part in the designing, too, but much more in the execution of the plan. And we still had lots of questions after the planning stage! Would I find in N'Djamena good lumber for the roof, windows and doors? Would I find in the village a good crew who could do the mud-brick walls and cement floor? Would my son Jonathan and I have the stamina to supervise building during the hottest time of the year? Like General Jackson's wagon-master, we were willing to give it a try with what was at our disposal.

Mud bricks were made for our house during the cooler days of November and December. The sun had plenty of time to harden them by the time my son and I came to start the building operation the following March. I did find good local builders and workers for putting up the basic structure. The two masons and their helpers were well used to building with mud-brick, yet there were some new wrinkles for them. We wanted our house to look as much as possible like the buildings around – but we had to have larger windows for more air and we needed screens to keep the mosquitoes out. Instead of the flatish mud roofs they used, we opted for a metal roof with more pitch. So they didn't have the fun of slinging balls of mud up to their camrades perched on palm trunk planks and woven palm mats who would then slap the mud into place on top! Instead they helped Jonathan and me lay out roof timbers to which sheets of aluminum were nailed. This was new for them and they seemed baffled by our concern that the timbers be carefully placed so many centimeters apart. Let's say they just didn't seem to understand the need for tape measures! They were a good crew, though, and they took the goofy ideas of the white man in stride.

Most of the house was built in a month. Part of that time coincided with the Muslim fast month of Ramadan. Though it was the hottest time of the year and the workers could not eat or drink during the daylight fast hours, they kept working – often having a jolly time together as they did! I gained a new respect for African manhood those days. They endured hardship that would have made their white brothers wilt! The myth that many from the West hold of lazy African men sitting in the shade of their working wives just didn't hold. Many other myths would blow away as we lived among African villagers in the next 10 years.

In November that year (1989) Ali Bah was moved to a new work location in Chad. Just a few days later we also moved to our new work. God timed that just right! We had contracted with a Mundang trucker to haul our household goods the 230 miles or so to our future home, but a few days before the date set for moving I came down with hepatitis. Could we start out as planned? We did! We started out early on the morning of November 15th – armed with lots of applesauce and cookies to keep the sugar level up as I drove our '78 Toyota Corolla station-wagon, loaded with the more vulnerable household items such as our gas kitchen stove. Our younger son, David, rode in the cab of the truck which was very loaded down. Space was at such a premium that we got the measurements of the truck-bed beforehand and planned where every larger item would be placed.

Almost 30 years before we had driven a short distance on this very road. Then, we had just arrived in Africa and were visiting the pioneer missionary couple who were at that time residing at Lere. Where had all those years gone? Our three children had now all grown up, but it was Lere where their roots were. Many happy and some hard and frustrating times for us all there. It was hardest for David to make the break with his childhood home. He had learned the local language the best and, though the youngest, had actually lived there the longest. Carolee was now living with her family in Cameroon – about a hundred miles to the north. Jonathan was living near N'Djamena, over 200 miles to the north. David came back to Chad twice to visit us during the 1980s after finishing his schooling in auto mechanics at a technical school and attending a Bible college. Realizing the great need for a full-time Christian book seller in the Lere area, he stayed on. And he would have liked to stay on in Lere and continue his book-selling work there. Even the Muslims were beginning to buy his Christian books before we left! So it was more of a sacrifice for him to leave Lere on that November morning than it was for Orpha and me.

As I drove the first several miles, Orpha read Psalm 121 – the traveler's Psalm – and then prayed for strength and protection on the way. We discovered we needed both! A couple hours later as we were traveling through a large town, a boy dashed out in front of our car and I missed him by a hair! If I had hit him, our chances of going to Mesken then – or ever – would have been slim! When, in late afternoon, we rolled into another large town where there was a customs post, we didn't anticipate any problem whatsoever. I had gone to the trouble to get a special permit, listing the objects that were on the truck. Normally, this would have satisfied any customs inspector. But not this one! He told us we needed to stay overnight, because our load needed to be checked carefully. No argument could change his mind. As we were pondering what to do, the youth pastor of our church there came along and invited us to stay the night at his place. He was a real encouragement to us. Though Mundang, he wanted us to go and work among the Muslims. We discovered that evening that a tourist couple from Germany had been shot at in an ambush a day or so previously on this very road we were planning to travel. The inspector did not have to go through our goods the next morning after all, but he did feel responsible for our safety and thus kept us from going on further that night. When we left the customs post the next morning, he had an armed soldier ride on the top of our load to discourage any bandits. We thanked God for that inspector!

About noon we arrived in Mesken. Delays the day before due to bad roads and a breakdown would have caused us to come in at midnight if we hadn't stopped at the customs post the night before. Coming in at noon was much better – we got to experience a welcome we shall never forget! Orpha had never seen Mesken and its people before now, but people left her in no doubt that she was very welcome. Old lady Bala, who would be our closest neighbor, ran and hugged Orpha the moment she got out of the car. Others crowded around us with big smiles on their faces. We heard many times: "Warga, warga!" ("Welcome, welcome!")

Moving the "troops" from Lere to Mesken wouldn't have been complete without the villagers crowding around as our belongings were unloaded. Some things looked pretty "battle-scarred" because of a lot of bumping around on rough roads. Yet, the villagers "oohed and "aahed" as one item after another came off the truck, thinking, I'm sure, that we had a lot of wonderful things. Our stuff was old and of not good quality, but once again we saw that wealth is a relative matter. We did have more than they, although I believe there might have been several fancier wardrobe closets and cupboards in the village than ours. One of our cupboards had been built by a former missionary out of packing boxes in 1938! (The date and name were on the back side.)

The chief's wife brought us our evening meal – and three

meals the next day! The villagers tried in every way to make us feel at home. And we did feel at home. We felt at peace with our surroundings from the start, a peace that endured for the entire time we lived in that village. We had found our niche for the next segment of our lives.

6
Settling into our Nest

I took a walk one early morning not long after we moved to Mesken. The scenic trail along the Loumia River was coming alive with birdsong. I stopped when I noticed a weaver bird's nest that had fallen to the ground. I was struck by the beautiful workmanship of that nest – how the grass had been twisted in and out in such a way as to ensure a sturdy and comfortable home for the weaver bird family. Around its entrance the grass was especially fine and soft. Who but God could create a tiny bird with the intelligence and instinct to use so well what it found in its surroundings for nest-building!

Visitors and first house at Mesken

After we moved in, there were plenty of things to do to make our little "nest" more comfortable. It was a far cry from our large burnt-brick house at Lere. We found, however, that the amount of space doesn't necessarily relate to contentment. We had all kinds of challenges in our new setting, but while we were meeting these challenges, we were content and happy. The western sun shown too brightly into our house, so we bought a large grass mat to hang over the entrance as a shade. We needed a place to receive guests, so we built a small lean-to of poles and grass mats. We needed to keep goats away from our house, so we put up a simple fence. We strung clothes-lines between trees. We made a wooden seat to sit on in our outhouse. We made a simple bath-house outdoors of grass mats placed in a circle. We put up barrels for collecting water that we at first hauled from the river. (Later, when we realized that the contamination level of river water was too high, we hauled water from a hand-pump three miles away.) I was weak for some weeks from the hepatitis that I had contacted a couple days before we moved in November and I was very grateful for the willing hands of our son and our neighbors during those settling-in days.

Before we built our house, the chief told me we could live anywhere we wanted in the village. I remember that I had looked around then and I had spotted a place right off the river on a bluff with many trees on it. I suggested that spot to the chief. "Well, that is the one place you can't build a house." he said. "That is our cemetery." So he then suggested a couple other sites and I decided on this one. It was a good site for langage learning and observing the sights. Paths going to the fields and the big market in a neighboring village passed right by that spot. So while we lived there, we saw and heard much people traffic – and horses, donkeys and, occasionally, camels, too. And neighbors lived only a few steps away.

There were other sounds in the compact village of which we were now a part. Roosters crowing, sheep and goats bleating. It sounded like one big farmyard! And then, of course, the Muslim call to prayer five times a day, beginning around 4:30 in the morning and ending around 8 in the evening. At those prayer times, stillness would descend on the 60-some households in the village, broken only by the chants of those praying. Some would pray inside or in front of the village mosque – especially on Fridays. For most of the people, though, the ten-minute prayers would be uttered at their homes – either just outside their homes, usually with several others, or inside their compounds. Muslim women pray, but I don't recall ever having seen one pray in public in Mesken. Their worship of God is supposed to be much more private than that of the menfolk. So their praying, I discovered, was confined to their homes.

We found our community to be a quiet and peaceful one. Alcohol is forbidden by the Islamic religion and from our beginning days in the village we were very grateful for that. No loud brawling and fighting due to drinking. In fact, raising one's voice seemed to be frowned upon for any reason. Dogs were noticably absent in the village. I thought at first because they made too much noise. Later, I realized that dogs were looked upon by Muslims as despicable animals; a good Muslim would never own one. In our early years in Mesken, we didn't hear singing in the village. That was different! When we lived among the Mundang, we would hear women sing while they pounded and ground their corn. Singing would often accompany dances. Christians would sing when they got together for worship. But in Mesken, only later, as some children began attending French school and learned secular songs there, did we hear any singing at all. (And we discovered that the children had beautiful voices!) But no other singing – and no drums or musical instruments, no dancing in the village. Music seemed to be something Muslims weren't interested in. Did it have something to do with influencing adversely the spirit realm? Or was it just considered frivolous? Or something that awakened evil desires in the heart? We had lots to learn in those early days.

7
Muslims and Magic

According to Scripture, there is a magic that is real – unlike that which merely entertains us who live in the Western world. Psychology may certainly play a role in the magical practices of the witchdoctor, but the powers of darkness are very much involved. We cannot laugh away as superstition the belief that demons exist and have power to do supernatural things – even today. Real demons wreaked havoc in Bible times. We have no reason to say they don't today. To counter this real demonic power, many people in the world still resort to magic such as an

amulet-maker and witchdoctor would use.

There was one in our village; we called him Al Haj. He was an uncle of the village chief and had been to Mecca – and thus had earned the right to use the title "Al Haj." He had gone on his "haj" (pilgrimage) in younger days. He impressed me early on in Mesken as one who wanted to help me learn the Bagirmi language.

Al Haj

27

One day, shortly after we had arrived in Mesken, Al Haj took me on a tour of some millet fields in the area. There were piles of millet here and there, waiting to be carried home. He pointed out the "precautions" he and others had taken against thievery by both two and four-footed creatures. I couldn't understand much of his language yet and I didn't know much Arabic either, but he managed to get across his message: "This hole here, look!" I did. I noticed a piece of paper lying in the foot-deep hole. "That paper protects the millet." "And see that stick over there?" I did, and saw a stick that may have had something tied to it, sticking up in the middle of a pile of millet. "That is guarding the millet-pile." Al Haj seemed to have complete confidence in the "precautions" against thievery.

I am sure that Al Haj regarded himself as a devout Muslim. But wasn't he hanging on to some real pagan ideas about the power of charms and amulets? Wasn't he trying to manipulate spirits? What he and his fellow Muslims seemed to be doing was to ignore God's power to protect, relying on their own devices to keep their millet intact! But what could a piece of paper do – even if it had a Quranic verse written on it? What could a stick do by itself to ward off thieves? When I ask those questions I am thinking like a white man schooled to dismiss the power of the spirit realm. Renaissance thinking has greatly influenced even us who have, we believe, an entirely Christian worldview. We tend to divide the world into two domains: spiritual and natural. The wall we have erected between them has often led to a denial, in practice, of the supernatural in everyday human life, whether we realize it or not. We usually look for purely physical or natural causes when one becomes sick or something is stolen or a house burns down. Not so among most people in the world. For the missionary, because of our background in Western secular thinking, it is sometimes hard to believe that the spirit realm can actually affect us in the here and now. We may dismiss belief in evil spirits as plain superstition; we may try to bring "civilized" ideas about germs and gravity and galaxies to the rest of the world who predominately believe in the power of the unseen forces – and miss our opportunities to witness to them of our God Who has concern for man's everyday needs and has power to "give good gifts to those who ask him!" When one is in league with evil spirits, they are indeed able to do things for the one who believes in them and performs the right rituals. They are very real – as those who have lived in non-Western cultures know. But the "gifts" that come from the evil spirits can hardly be called "good!" They lead to terrible bondage.

Al Haj was more than a believer in witchcraft – that is, a believer in the power of amulets or charms – he was actually the one in the village who made them. He offered them for sale to ward off evil effects – trouble of any kind – caused by witches, jinns or demons. He was also very knowledgeable about herbs and the bark, roots and leaves of trees. He used them, too, to attack evil forces – with the proper chants and rituals over them, I assume. Some of these may have had medicinal powers in them with or without the rituals and therefore could heal someone of sickness on their own. But coming to Al Haj for help even with these would lay one open to demonic powers as long as the rituals were done over them. I believe Al Haj really thought of himself as a doctor who brought good to people and not just an opportunist – although he certainly at times seemed to be just that!

When we first came into contact with Bagirmi Muslims, we were surprised to see the extent to which they clung to animistic beliefs – that is, belief in the ability to manipulate spirits. Didn't these people believe in God? Wasn't Islam, along with Christianity and Judaism, among the three religions in the world who professed belief in the one Creator God Who didn't share His power with others? How then could they be so taken up with trying in their own ways to cope with demonic forces? We learned that, yes, they confessed the greatness of Allah many times a day, but the fact was they lived in real fear of evil spirits. These "shaytans", as they called them, were everywhere – the word was often on their lips. Actually, the Bagirmi Muslims were no different in this respect than maybe 80 percent or more of the Muslims in the world who are preoccupied with demonic forces and how to control them. These people are followers of what is called folk-Islam. To orthodox Muslims, folk-Islam is idolatrous. Many of the extremists or radicals among the Muslims today would be considered among the more orthodox followers of Islam who pride themselves on taking the Quran more seriously than others. They scorn those who follow what they believe is a perverted form of Islam. Some of today's Muslim terrorists are among these. They want to purge the world of what they consider a poor grade of Islam. So they'll even kill fellow-Muslims – as well as the "infidels" who aren't Muslims – because they're not following Allah the way Muhammad taught. Muhammad would have cheered them on! He very much believed in force to coerce people to follow his religion. Yet, he himself wavered on the point of falling back on witchcraft. He allowed, for example, certain magical practices or spells – to counteract such things as the "evil eye" and snake bites. And he exhorted people to touch the black stone in their sacred shrine in Mecca in order to get a special blessing, believing it contained great magical powers.

Al Haj was definitely one of the power brokers in Mesken because he was – in the minds of the populace – indispensable to their well-being. Yet, I often saw that he did not mix much with the people. There was another man – besides the village chief – who also wielded a lot of power – and I saw this man usually surrounded by people. He, too, was looked upon as absolutely indispensable.

8
The Imam

Malla Hassa was the imam in Mesken. He was the one who was expected to lead and keep people on the right path. It was he who was the preserver and the explainer of the Islamic traditions. His powers were linked with the Quran, fasting, memorizing Quranic verses and leading the prayers – especially at weddings, funerals, name-giving ceremonies and special holidays. As far as I know, he did not delve into magical practices. Nor did he spend a lot of time exhorting his people to not follow them – although I could be mistaken. He and Al Haj, the magic practitioner, seemed to be on opposite sides, and although I never heard them speak against each other and their respecte ways of dealing with life's needs and problems, they were seldom seen together in the village. People seemed to highly respect Malla Hassa, the imam. He stood for the "real" Islam. Al Haj, though, was needed. People believed he knew the secrets of fending off the attacks of evil forces.

Shortly before we left Lere to go to Mesken, a widow with 10 children came to our house. Her pastor husband had been dead for several years and she was doing her best to keep her family together. She was a godly woman who had a special concern for children and had been very active in Sunday School work. She felt that we were making a big mistake in moving away to work with Muslims – and she had come that day to tell us so. I reminded her of the importance of knowing the Word of God. Didn't I bring much help to her that day she came to our house soon after her husband passed away? She was so despondent that day; she didn't know how to cope with raising a family alone. But I had then shown her a couple of verses in the Mundang Bible – Proverbs 3: 5 and 6: "Trust in the Lord with all your heart and lean not on your own understanding. In all your ways acknowledge Him and He will direct your steps."

Yes, as I reminded her of that day some years before, she had to admit that God's Word really had helped her then. I asked her, "So now, what about those other people whom God also loves who have no Bible to help them – not even a single page?" That hit home! After a moment, she replied, "Yes, go." "Go, try and reach the Muslim children." Esther had little or no faith that the adults could be won to Christ, but if we started with the children, maybe we could someday reach the adults through them. So we got her blessing on going to the Muslims!

The dear widow was right in her zeal for reaching children; we realized though when we came to Mesken, that we could not begin our Muslim work by first trying to win the children. We would not have been tolerated in the village very long if people knew that we were trying to get their children away from what they had always believed. Their religion was closely connected with everything else and they couldn't be Bagirmi people without following what their forefathers always believed. To them, to leave Islam was to cease being a member of their tribe and all that was familiar and dear to them.

From the start, I spent much time with those men who held the reins of power in the village. I needed to win over their confidence, first. I invited Al Haj to help me with his language, witchdoctor or not! He would come over each morning. Sometimes we would walk together in the countryside and he would tell me the names of all sorts of grasses, trees and herbs, pointing out to me how each was useful. (I'm sure he kept some of his knowledge to himself, though!) One time he came over with a small turtle and we observed its antics – and I learned some useful words that way. Other times he would come over with an old object – a fishhook, a spear point, some canoe paddle that needed fixing – and we would talk as we observed and repaired. He was really quite a good teacher. One day I received a list of Bagirmi words from Pauline, one of the WEC missionaries who lived a hundred miles to the south. That list was very useful in the early days as I could then have Al Haj pronounce and define the words and I could make more rapid progress than if I had to ferret out each word in the language as I first had to do.

To understand Islamic vocabulary is important to one who wants to witness to Muslims and to translate any of God's Word in their language. For this the imam was very helpful. I would often sit with Malla Hassa and ask him to explain Bagirmi religious terms, which were always Arabic words, I found out. We would discuss such terms as "sin", "prayer", "fasting", "creation", and "prayer beads". One day when the village needed rain badly and I told him that I was asking God to send rain, he was surprised that a white man, too, would pray to God for rain and then he asked me if I used "wirde" (prayer beads) when I prayed. He was puzzled to hear that I didn't and even more so when I told him that I talked to God as I would talk to people here on earth: "I just talk to God with my mouth." For him, it was not that simple! Malla Hassa would try to explain a lot of things to me, especially when I began to do some simple Bible translation and wanted to know the meaning in his language of certain words. There was much I missed, though, because of my lack of skill in his language. But I much appreciated his efforts to teach me. I suppose his aim, though, was really to convert me to Islam!

I discovered that the chief's son, Idi, was also willing to help me with the language from time to time. When we first came to Mesken he was almost twenty and he knew some French – because he was of the chief's household and was permitted to go to the "white man's school". He helped me translate some simple things from the Bible after I had learned the language a little. One of these was a description of the ostrich (Job 4). This was of interest to the villagers because there was an ostrich at that time in the chief's compound. We also worked on some simple sayings in the Book of Proverbs. The Bagirmi love riddles and proverbs. Later we worked on the story of Joseph in the Book of Genesis. This was interesting to people because the story of Joseph is the most complete of any Bible story in the Quran – but they discovered the Bible had many additional details that the Quran did not contain. We also translated the parable of the prodigal or lost son in Luke 15 – a story that Idi and others loved.

One day I and some men of the village were sitting with the

imam in his favorite spot just outside his home. At one point Malla Hassa turned to the men and said something like this: "Our people need to hear what this man (referring to me) is bringing to our village. We need to know the *Tawrat* (Books of Moses), the *Zabur*, (Psalms of David), and the *Injil* (Sayings of Jesus)." I was surprised and grateful to God to hear these words from the highly respected imam. If there were those who were wary of me and of what I was beginning to read to them from the Bible, from that point on they would be less so. After all, if the imam says something is okay, who would argue with him?

As surely as Ali Bah, Saleh Moda, and Blama Hassan, the chief, were chosen by God to help us get into Mesken village, so were Al Haj, Malla Hassa, and Idi, the chief's son, chosen by Him to help us get established in the language and the actual work of getting God's Word to the Bagirmi people. "Something wonderful is going on here!" I wrote in my journal one of those early days after meditating on what God was doing.

9
The Ladder

Having lived most of my life overseas, I enjoy reading about Americans. What makes Americans "tick" and how much have I been influenced by my roots? The Pacific Northwest was home to me for 12 of my most impressionable years before going to Africa; thus, when I came across an analysis one day that a researcher made of people living in that corner of America, I was interested. She found that the people there tended to divide their world into three broad categories. The first included the world of nature, weather, politics, sports and other events over which most people feel they have little control. Casual conversations generally operated in this category. The second included possessions which people owned to do whatever needed doing – tools and things such as tractors, livestock, pencils, books, chairs, beds, clothes and houses. The third category were people to whom those researched related in some way. These were seen as thinking, feeling and caring people like themselves. The shocking finding was that the people she researched did not see all humans as "people." Strange and foreign humans they really saw as "scenery." Like things in the first category. One talks about them and even with them, but always on a very casual level and never to the point of getting involved with them and their world. Then some, like Mexican migrant laborers, were seen as useful "machinery" – like things in the second category. But the only people that these Americans saw as "real" were those who were family and friends! The missionary, if he is not careful, can easily treat people from different cultures as though they are interesting – and sometimes stupid – followers of strange customs and religions and they may be treated little better than "scenery." And those who work with and for the missionary may be treated as little more than useful "machines". In Africa we were continually challenged to see all people as real people and that would include those walking around in white gowns and praying in strange ways or those who eat with their fingers from a common platter on the ground and talk with strange sounds!

There was a good steel ladder that seemed to sort of "float" around the village. It could be seen popping up in almost anyone's compound and we never did know to whom it belonged. There were other things like that – wheelbarrows, crowbars, spades and wrenches. We from the West want to keep track of the tools we lend out – they are ours, aren't they? We noticed that Mesken villagers looked upon possessions in a somewhat different manner. It seemed like many things belonged to the entire village – and people were free to use something and keep it as long as they needed it. Because they kept such a close eye on each other, they apparently had little trouble knowing who had what at any given time. We discovered that we weren't able to live that close to them, so on the numerous times they asked to use our tools, we had a much harder time to keep track of which tool was where!

This brings up something else. When villagers at any time heard that we were driving to N'Djamena for mail or supplies, the word got around quickly and often someone would come to our house and say, "I'm going to N'Djamena with you." When I first heard this way of making a request, I felt like saying, "Oh, you think so, do you?" But I did want to treat them like real people and not things, and so I would politely tell them that it would not be possible this time – if we couldn't for some reason take them. Often we had empty fuel containers or butane gas cannisters to take along and our space was limited. But when we could, we would take one or two along with us without charging them, which was more than those driving pick-ups for hauling people would do. But we discovered that the people around us never liked to have us say No! One of the hardest things about living in Africa, we found, is that we Americans who tend to be direct to people find it hard to lie and agree to something if we know we can't perform a service. To them, it's better to agree to something and then break the agreement.

People then wouldn't have to bear the shame of being turned down!

Competition is something that is learned and encouraged from a very early age in America. In an African village, however, cooperation and harmony are valued much more. That has been changing to some extent in recent years as soccer games and school exams are part of modern life for many young people. Jobs in the big cities or on the oil fields in Chad are for the most qualified and there is stiff competition to get them. There is much more interplay now between tribes than there was 30 years ago. In the past it was okay to beat a person from another tribe or race out of something (they weren't considered "real" people!), but not someone from your own tribe. Nowadays, because they are more used to mixing with outsiders, they are more competitive when among their own, too. But in the old days and to some extent, still, in the small villages like Mesken, there was less competition between tribal members. They would tend to act together as a group, sharing time and resources with others. Numerous proverbs or tribal sayings among African tribes show this solidarity spirit: "It takes two sticks of wood to make a good fire." "You wash your hands by rubbing two hands together." "It takes two thumbs to squash a louse."

Sitting with the men in the village, I tried to pick up clues to the way they thought and acted in differing circumstances. I made many mistakes. I would walk fast sometimes, and I was told that older men, especially, never do that – except while in a group taking a body to the burial ground, I noticed. Then they almost run! I have been known to have cleaned dirt off my sandals or my feet with my right hand. That's bad. The right hand and the left hand each has specific functions and one better know which to use when! One doesn't whistle. One doesn't step on a mat with sandals on. I would be too time-oriented. While visiting with men, I had to learn to sit and sit. Relationships and friendships were far more important there than most anything else.

I found that the villagers were very tolerant of us. We could make mistakes and even hurt their feelings, but there was always another day. The fact that we were not foreigners who came for quick visits and left again, but lived with them year after year, sharing their joys and sorrows even on what must have been at a rather shallow level, made a great difference. We were like family in some important ways. Our connection with the villagers took on more and more that of "real" people – real in the sense that the Pacific Northwest people in that research study looked upon those who were friends and relatives. There were times, however, when we did feel like we were being "used" by the villagers – and also that we were "scenery" to them when our peculiar ways of doing things made them gape at us as if we were animals in a zoo. Yet, they had feelings concerning what is proper and they tended to mask their surprise at our antics.

Young belles of the village

10
A Religion Without Song

The great missionary to the Muslims of nearly a century ago, Samuel Zwemer, once described orthodox Islam as "a religion without song." Their idea of God is "conspicuously lacking in the attribute of love," he wrote. How different from the Bible where love is not just an attribute of God – He is love! He can never do anything outside of love. The human heart is not satisfied with a loveless God – it longs for a God Who can be touched with the feeling of our infirmities and Who hears and answers our prayers. About such a God, the Quran is silent! I have been impressed many times with the lack of joy while Muslims worship. Instead of song rising from their lips at such times, there are grim faces and groanings. It's as if the more they can feel the harshness of their religion, the more their Allah is pleased! "Allah is too rich and too proud and too independent to need or desire the tribute of human love. In consequence Islam is a loveless creed," Zwemer wrote. When a being is incapable of loving as their Allah is, then he is incapable of being loved by His creatures. I have more than once, though, detected a wistfulness about those who listen to the stories of God's love in the Old Testament or the loving ways in which Jesus treated people in the New. It's as though they are thinking that they could love God if He were like that, but alas! He isn't – or so their religion tells them!

In Islam, God stands completely separate and aloof from His creation. One has said that Muhammad teaches a God above us, Moses teaches a God above us and yet with us, and Jesus reveals a God Who is above us, with us , and in us. And He teaches that God is above us as a Heavenly Father, not as an oppressive despot. The idea of God being likened to a father is blasphemy to orthodox Muslims. It puts God down at the level of human beings, they say. The proper way to approach Allah is to consider oneself as a slave who has no will of his own. Allah decides all and thus a person is not held responsible. Not even Adam can be held accountable; Allah created Adam weak and with sensuous appetites and thus it was only natural that he should fall – he couldn't have done otherwise. Those coming after Adam are basically good, although, unfortunately, weak and forgetful of God's commands. So we don't need salvation, they say, we only need guidance, and Islam offers that! After Adam sinned, Allah simply forgave him and assured him that if he followed the guidance found in the Quran, he would have nothing to fear.

Jesus Christ, then, is not needed as a savior; to Muslims, He is only a man – though a great one, second only to Muhammad. Muslims have a very faulty idea of the holiness of God. Though He is unspeakably great and powerful, as we would agree, He can easily overlook His laws and show leniency to a repentant Muslim sinner without any kind of sin-offering paid. His time in a purgatory-like place of suffering may be shortened (especially if his deeds throughout life are found on the Day of Judgment to have been over 50 percent good) and he will most likely make it some day to paradise. But the only one who can be absolutely sure of going to paradise immediately after death is the one who dies a martyr's death while on a jihad for the Muslim faith – a suicide bomber, for instance, who kills the infidels. The infidels include the Jews and Christians – there is no chance of them ever getting into paradise. Even to the faithful Muslim, the way to God's mercy is never really sure. One can hope and that's about it. There are many "perhaps", "ifs" and "maybes" along the way. Except for the suicide bomber; he will for sure go to paradise – and to the highest place at that.

11
More Building Days

Our first dwelling in the village was getting a bit small for the three of us. We were showing symptoms of "cabin fever" at times. The lean-to of poles and grass mats tumbled down with a heavy early rain in our second rainy season and we then had still less space for living. I knew we had to begin another building project that dry season. Not long before we started, I found in Psalms 86:11 a prayer that I made my own: "Teach me your way, O Lord... give me an undivided heart." Along with that, I found that the fourth stanza of an ancient hymn expressed my thoughts well:

> *"Direct, control, suggest this day,*
> *All I design, or do, or say,*
> *That all my powers, with all their might.*
> *In Thy sole glory may unite."*
> *- "Awake, My Soul, and with the Sun"*

We needed God's guidance for all kinds of activities those early days and it was a relief to turn to God for this kind of help. I don't think the Muslims around us knew anything about this sort of thing. To them the petition, "Thy kingdom come, Thy will be done" is blasphemy. Allah will do what He wills regardless of our prayers, Muslims say. And yet, I discovered that the villagers petitioned Allah for rain and asked His blessings on their new-born infants. There were many things I didn't understand! There seemed to be inconsistencies and contradictions in Islam.

Our second dwelling of 15 by 32 feet went up quickly. On February 23, 1992, we had a Chadian "house-warming" celebration to dedicate our new building to God. The chief helped me pick out the two sheep for the event, the young men

41

of the village butchered and roasted them and made lots of tea, the chief's wife bought condiments and other food items, such as rice, that she and other women cooked up in large quantities, Orpha made lots of cookies, and everyone in the village was invited to come and help us celebrate. Like so many Muslim celebrations, though, it was the men and older boys that showed up – the men sitting on the cement flour of our newly white-washed house and the boys sitting outside. Before the women sent off the best portions of food with young men who came to get it, they managed to keep a little for themselves. So typically Muslim – the men celebrate and the women are left to fend for themselves in a catch-as-catch-can fashion. In the Muslim paradise, too, the women get short shrift – it is almost exclusively the domain of the male gender; only a few very special women seem to get in! We didn't want to neglect the women like this, but it was their way and they were more comfortable with it. I read the Lord's Prayer from my Chad Arabic Testament to those who came. Not all understood, but probably most. The oldest son of the iman went out of his way to thank me for doing that.

One day, shortly before the rains came that year, we sat on the stoop of our new house and watched 33 baby chameleons

Our second house

climb out of a small hole in the ground, each following close behind the other. They all headed for a couple palm trees just beyond the stoop. They climbed them as if they knew exactly what they were doing and where they wanted to go – no indecision! Several days later, we were treated to quite a show of camel stubbornness. One man was trying to get three camels to get on their way. They, too, knew exactly what they wanted and they let their master know by loud bellows. They wanted to keep sitting, but the man persisted and finally won out. Another day, we saw around 100 camels pass close by our home, accompanied by several herders. The baby camels were more legs than anything and they were very awkward-looking as they tried to keep up with the herd. We were building up a store of information on local animal life...

We were learning about canoes, also. I loved to watch men make the dugouts. One day one of the better canoe-builders and his sons were working on an unpromising-looking log – far from straight and with two large holes where the bottom of the canoe would be. Tahir was undaunted by the challenge. I wrote in my journal: "If they can make something out of this that floats well, then it certainly is to their credit – the raw material cannot get the credit! And if God can make something of me, certainly that must be to His credit and not mine!"

"I'll teach you my language, but I am not interested in you reading or talking about Jesus." I had just read 17 simple Bible stories to Al Haj. They were something we had composed in Bagirmi in an attempt to introduce some basic Christian truths. After I read to Al Haj that morning, I tried to explain to him again that we hadn't come to his village to collect language data and other information about his people so that we could then return to America and sell what we had collected. (Years ago an American ethnologist had done just that. He and his family had lived for several years in a village just a little ways up the river from us.) Al Haj was wary of Americans! He didn't want us to make money off his people. I told him that all I really wanted was for him to know Jesus and tried to show him why that is so important. That is when he told me he didn't want to hear any more on that subject. I believe it was then that he left in a huff and didn't come again to our house for many weeks.

I think it was not long after that when we decided that it would be better to stick only to translating actual Bible texts instead of composing Bible stories. It was an important decision! In the Muslim milieu we were living in, we could then say that what we were reading to them was what the Bible actually said and to them this would have more authority. After three years into working with the Bagirmi people, we were probably still largely influenced by what we did for 30 years while working among Christian families. We still had plenty to learn about working with Muslims!

A few months later, Malla Hassa, the imam died! He had been taken to N'Djamena for treatment for an illness several days previously. At siesta time (early afternoon) when all would normally be quiet in the village, his body was taken back to his home. An awful wailing suddenly erupted and we quickly learned why. Soon the village would be full of people as neighboring villages heard the news. It was a large funeral – probably the largest the village had seen in decades. His body was buried the same day as it was brought to the village, but people kept coming from more distant areas over the next couple of days. There was lots of eating, formal group praying and quiet sitting on mats for a number of days after the body had been buried. I and many others felt a loss when the imam died. I spent a lot of time with the mourners those days. Two adult sons of the imam noticed this and showed their gratefulness to me. I believe it was the beginning of a good relationship that continued up to the day we left their village over seven years later.

Building a house was not a big deal among the Bagirmi as it often is among Americans. A few days would generally suffice for that. But building relationships was another story altogether. That can take years and to their way of thinking, well worth the time spent! We were beginning to think like them. We wanted more than anything to be known as their friends who really cared about them. If our roof leaked a little or the bathroom facilities were not up to par or the inside mud walls of our house needed another coat of whitewashing, working on these needed to be weighed against time spent making friends and reading to them the Bible. We were trying to keep eternity's values in view.

12
An Important Man Comes to Town

Sometimes important moments appear with very little fanfare, very little to indicate at the time that something big is about to happen. A day in June of 1993 started out as any other day. That morning I walked to a favorite sitting place of men, looking forward to a little more relationship-building. When I arrived, there was a stranger sitting with the other men. I found myself sitting down on a mat next to him. Quickly I discovered that he could talk rather good French. As he shared a little bag of peanuts with me, he told me that he had come back to his home village after living in N'Djamena for 20 years where he had worked at the central pharmacy depot there. But he wasn't planning to be in the village very long – maybe a month or so. He had come in hope of getting some traditional medicine for his eyes, he said. He was almost totally blind, having been hurt in a motorcycle accident several years before.

Kusu (pronounced "Coo-Sue") wasn't going to be doing much in the short time he would be in the village. Because of his blindness, he would be mostly sitting while others went out into their fields at this busy time of the year. My mind began working. Perhaps he would be available for some language help that I still needed! I had never had a language helper who knew as much French as he and maybe I could make some rapid strides in the Bagirmi language – even if he could only help me a month. I asked him. Sure, he said, he would be willing to help me. So began both morning and afternoon language learning sessions with Kusu.

He was still in the village a month later. I asked him if he would translate the story of the Good Samaritan for me. He agreed and he did a good job of it and seemed to enjoy the work. By that time I was really hoping that he could stay longer and translate much more for me. Idi, the chief's son, was still helping

46

me at that time and we were working on a long story that we later used for one of the literacy booklets. But his knowledge of French was limited – and he would be soon leaving for more schooling in N'Djamena. We had been praying for someone to replace Idi, not having a clue who that person could be.

When we pray, God often sends us something better than we asked for! Two months went by, then three – and there was no more talk from Kusu about leaving the village. When I asked him if he would be willing to keep translating portions from the Bible, he seemed eager to do so. So we worked on stories from the Gospel of Luke, especially. Because he was no longer able to read due to his blindness, I would have to read a short sentence or phrase to him in French and then as he translated, I would write this down. I would often have to explain a word or expression and there would be discussion and rereadings. Sometimes the next day he would say that he had been thinking of what we had translated the day before and he felt that the word or expression could be improved. So he would come with a better word or expression. Kusu wanted the translation to be accurate!

Four months after Kusu arrived in the village, I was ready to attempt translating the Passion and Resurrection passages at the end of Luke's Gospel. The big question was: What about Kusu, was he ready? One morning we discussed for a long time the subject of a person making a sacrifice for someone else's sin. There are several doctrines that the Muslim holds on to very tenaciously and one of them is that no one can be judged in the place of another – there is no such thing as a sacrifice in that sense. I told Kusu what the death of Jesus meant to me. I could go free because Jesus sacrificed His life in my place. I knew this whole section of Luke's Gospel is foolishness to the Muslim – in fact, to them it is actually blasphemous. They say Allah is there depicted as one who is so weak that he couldn't have prevented his second greatest prophet from dying a humiliating death. Kusu was a good Muslim and he knew his Quran very well. How would he regard translating this section? I felt it was important before we launched into this section of Luke to give Kusu a preview of what we would be next translating – if he agreed.

47

I then asked him if he would be willing to translate this material. I was greatly relieved when he said that he would, even though these teachings were not in the Quran. He said that translating this would not affect his own faith. He had one stipulation, though. Whenever anyone was around, we should not translate this section because he did not want others to hear what we were translating. I agreed to that. The next morning there were people around both morning and afternoon and so we translated the story of the Tower of Babel instead.

The next several weeks we made slow progress on the Passion and Resurrection part of Luke. We usually sat outside in plain view of passersby and often one or several of these would sit down and listen. That was usually great, because others would hear God's Word that way and would occasionally make comments. We finally reached the end of Luke one day in November while there was hardly a soul in the village. We had put in a long, hard morning of work. I noticed that Kusu had seemed somewhat agitated while working that morning – was he afraid that somebody had overheard us? Yet, when I mentioned the time that we quit working, he remarked, "The time went very fast." It is quite possible that Kusu had been totally absorbed in and even greatly moved by the tremendous story of Christ's death and resurrection!

Several days later, on a Sunday morning, Kusu and I had a long talk about Jesus and the salvation He offers. I read several verses from here and there in the New Testament in French. In fact, when we would get into such subjects, we would usually use French, because I could express myself much better in that language. I explained that Jesus is like the sheep that Abraham offered to God in the place of his son, Isaac. I asked him what he thought about all the references in the Quran to the material delights in paradise but none to the spiritual. We even got into the subject of the Trinity. Muslims have quite a time with that doctrine and I don't think I made much headway explaining it to Kusu that day!

Those first few months with Kusu were wonderful. Little did I know then that I would have almost six more years of interaction with him. He proved to be a very important man.

13

"The Words of Jesus Are Good!"

Christmas Day came that year and Kusu was still in Mesken. That morning I sat with him in the village and we talked about the justice of God. Why did Jesus come into the world and die like a criminal anyway? Was that necessary? Muslims are baffled by our ideas of Jesus and Kusu was no exception. I pointed out to him that morning that there would be no justice if sin were not punished. If a president of a country hands out pardons to criminals without exacting any kind of punishment, would we respect him? If not, how then can we respect God if we say He is lenient towards the sinner and simply forgives without someone having to suffer the consequences? I went on to explain that God had to punish sin by death and that the death of His Son is the only Sacrifice for sin that He can accept because the sin-offering has to be one that completely pleases Him.

A little later that same Christmas Day, I was reading back to Kusu what we had translated on a section of the Sermon on the Mount found in chapter 6 of the Gospel of Luke. We came to verses 35 and 36. There, Jesus was telling His listeners that they should love their enemies and do good to them. A friend of Kusu's, a teacher of the Quran to young boys, was sitting nearby and was listening closely. When I reached the part where Jesus states that the Most High is kind to the ungrateful and wicked, this teacher blurted out, "The words of Jesus are good!"

What I had just read was a far cry from Islamic theology! Muslims don't believe that we should love our enemies – we should rather crush them! They don't believe that Allah is ever merciful and loving towards the wicked, including all the infidels who don't believe in the Quran. Allah hates them and is determined to rid the world of such evil men! Why, then, did this devout Muslim teacher say that the words of Jesus are good when they contradict so strongly two main beliefs of Muslims?

I think this man was expressing – maybe without even thinking what he was really saying – the cry in his heart for such a God as Jesus taught. At any rate, he knew these words were good – even if they were against the Quran!

Blind Kusu and friend

14
Mr. Fix-It

One day a neighbor lady came over with her radio, complaining that she couldn't move a certain switch anymore. By this time our son David had gained a reputation for fixing things. Another time this same lady had come over with a noodle-making machine and he had fixed that. David opened up the short-wave radio and found it to be full of cockroaches. Not only that, but there was a lizard inside that had obviously been eating its fill of them. It had entered the radio while still small, but after all those meals, it had grown and couldn't get out. So the solution to this problem was simple – David removed the lizard and the cockroaches and the switch worked fine!

"Daa-veed!" There was someone yelling for our son again! What this time? Maybe a wristwatch band needed repairing – or a mouse-trap, or a bicycle brake, or a tire-pump, or a clock, or a wheelbarrow. Or someone needed a hammer or a saw or some other tool. Or some boys wanted to play soccer and wanted the ball pumped up. Or someone needed a dash of grease to make his bicycle wheels work after he'd washed the bicycle in the river and in the process washed away all the grease. Or some old woman needed a stick of wood she saw lying in our yard. Or a bit of kerosene to make her lamp burn again. Or some old motor-oil to stop the work of termites around her door. Or she needed to get her door open – she had locked her door with the key inside again! David was handy to have around – maybe too handy at times! He was a busy man in the village.

There were many times, I'm sure, when David felt relieved to be out on the road selling books. This was really his main work. Several days each week, especially during the dry seasons, he would visit markets – sometimes as far as 40 miles away, but more often closer. For the short distances he would usually use the bicycle that I bought for our children in 1964. Somehow he was able to keep that going year after year! For the longer trips he would drive his small Honda motorcycle. On these market trips he would sell both school supplies and Christian literature. Often he would get into interesting conversations – in various languages! Muslims would come around and look curiously at the Christian books and sometimes buy them if they were in Arabic or Fulani. David could handle both those languages enough for sales and small talk. Bibles and Testaments in a variety of other languages, too, were laid out on his selling mat, as well as books on the Christian life and on how to win Muslims to Christ. The latter two categories were usually in the French language. Many of those markets are on the main highway going from N'Djamena to southern Chad, and Christians who had emmigrated from the south years ago live in many of the villages along this highway. David saw that they badly needed Christian literature and determined to do something about it.

From the start David deliberately refrained from selling books to the Bagirmi in Mesken village. The Mesken men warned their children and young people to stay away from the books he sold in a market two miles away. But he did sell to many others who came to buy his attractive books in various languages at that market. After a while the Mesken fathers began wondering: Why weren't there any books in their language? After all, other tribes had books. David had to tell them that there weren't any yet!

One night David had his bicycle parked as usual just out-side his bedroom door – maybe a yard from his bed. It was loaded with books for the next book-trip. When he awoke in the morning, the bicycle was gone! We notified the village chief and he got several of his men together quickly and they started a search. Tracking animals was second nature to those men and following the tracks of the bicycle wasn't any big challenge to them. At one spot they found some of the books dumped off. When Blama Hassan noticed the kind of load that was on David's bicycle, he remarked, "It must be a Christian thief!" He and his men really felt badly for David and his loss and did what they could to catch the thief. But when the tracks ended at the Loumia River, their tracking skills didn't help. They knew the bicycle had been lifted aboard a canoe and taken up the river to who knows where. Several days later, however, someone in another village had spotted a man with David's bicycle and had notified the gendarmes. The thief was caught and beaten and David got his bike and most of his belongings back again. We were glad the thief was not a Bagirmi person and I'm sure the chief was too. As far as we know, this is the only time that anything was ever stolen from us during the ten years we lived in Mesken village.

We had an old 1982 French station-wagon with a diesel engine. At Wahpeton, N.Dak. where David had taken auto mechanics, he had not gotten into diesels, but he learned quite a few of a diesel engine's peculiarities as he got his hands under the hood on numerous occasions! Sometimes the problems were beyond his ability to fix, but The Great Fixer came to our aid again and again.

One of those times was when we were driving home from a missionary conference and the road was long and the day was fleeting. We came into an area where bushes grew close along the highway. It was not a good place; we thought of bandits. Then our car engine sputtered and we came to a stop. Well, this had happened a few times before with this car. David thought he knew the problem – most likely the fuel filter was clogged by dirty fuel and needed to be cleaned. So we cleaned it out. But in the process. we dropped a very important washer that prevented air from entering the fuel filter. It fell into the engine and try as we might, we could not find it. It would soon be dark and this was not a place to spend the night! We must have all prayed, but still no washer in sight. Suddenly Orpha, who has never claimed to be a diesel engine expert, asked, "Why don't you wrap this rubber band around the place where the washer should be?" We did, and we were soon on our way. The rubber band served very nicely until we could buy a new washer many miles and a few days later.

In Chad we didn't have handy service stations or medical clinics around the corner and so we were often put into positions where the only thing we could do was pray. Sometimes I wonder – is life too easy in America and is that why God often doesn't seem as close to us here? There is nothing like experiences with The Great Fixer to keep our dependency on God alive. "For when I am weak, then I am strong," the apostle Paul once wrote.

Mr. Fix-It was often frustrated while he worked on cars at the Wahpeton school. There, instead of fixing old parts and putting them back on cars again, he was taught to replace the old with new parts. That was not what he was used to ever since childhood. To him, it was far more interesting and less expensive to fix the old. He has had lots of chances in Mesken and on market roads to do it his way! His old Honda motorcycle and his 40-year-old bicycle know well his tinkering hands. So do a host of objects in the village.

15
Bright-Colored Folders

One night I had a dream. An elderly couple who we knew in the village had become Christians. In the dream they were very happy, rejoicing that they had found salvation through Christ. I never forgot that dream, nor did I forget old Ada and his wife. I prayed for them many times in the years that followed.

Vivid dreams are hard to forget. Many Muslims who have turned to Christ because of vivid dreams can tell us that! God uses dreams to stir people to do things they wouldn't otherwise do.

God Who speaks through dreams gave us an idea how to arouse the curiosity of our illiterate neighbors. Why not print stories in Bagirmi on bright-colored folders? I could then take these folders and read them to people in the village. We had been wondering how to get Bible truths to the villagers and this seemed to be the answer. In the early days in Mesken, Idi, the chief's oldest son, helped us get started by translating simple stories from the Bible. He was generally enthusiastic about doing this. A sensitive and feeling person, he seemed to think these stories would be good for his people to know. He, himself, was touched by them, I believe. We would sometimes get into good discussions as we worked together. As we got texts translated, Orpha would print them by hand on large, bright-colored folders and I started taking these around in my walks through the village.

Many were the times when I would sit down with a group of men with my folders of stories at my side. I generally would wait until one of them asked me to read from them. (Their bright colors helped to draw attention!) I noticed that old Ada was one who often asked me to do that. He would listen attentively, sometimes repeating my words – maybe thinking that was the way to get special blessing from them. Or to better remember the story.

Ada's older brother died one night. Jibiya had been a good neighbor of ours and had listened to me reading Bible texts, but not as avidly as his brother, Ada. That morning, I sat with the older men in mourning, reading one Bible text after another, the village chief urging me on. I often did this at such times because it was a time when men were especially open to hearing biblical truth. Ada missed his older brother very much, it seemed. After he died, Ada told me, "It's like my house has fallen down."

Translating and reading the Scriptures to people was very important, we knew. But we wanted more. We wanted people to have books for themselves and be able to read from them. We thought of the growing number of children in Mesken attending French-school in the mid-1990s. It seemed that more and more parents realized they could not keep their children from going to school. Education was the door to good jobs and jobs meant money – money that might help the parents in their old age. But we wanted people to get interested in reading in their own language. So we prayed.

One day I was sitting reading the story of the Prodigal Son out of one of our folders to several men. A man from another tribe who all the villagers knew came along just then. He had a job up the road a ways. The villagers knew he didn't speak their language. This man did know how to read in his own language, but of course had never read a book in the Bagirmi language. When he saw us, he wanted to see if he could read what was on the folder I had in my hands. He stood behind me – and started reading! His pronunciation left something to be desired, but it was good enough so that the men realized he was reading in their language. How was that possible? What kind of magic was this? Because he knew how to read in another language or two, he could make something out of the marks on the paper. The value of the letters could be translated from one language to another. No magic at all! I believe the men were impressed – whether or not they believed it was magic!

One of the first in the village who fervently wanted to learn to read was Blama Hassan, the village chief. He probably heard about that man who could read their language without knowing how to speak it. Blama Hassan was determined to get ahold of that power! As I started preparing literacy materials, he was among the first to try out our new reading system. I went through several pages with him. Then several other younger adults became interested. It was the beginning of Bagirmi literacy classes in our village!

We wanted to see what Mesken children could do. Because a number of them by now had started going to the village French-school and were learning French there, we were sure that they could make much better progress in reading than the adults. But how could we have literacy classes in a school that was run

Part of my literacy class

by the government? We knew that if we could, classes would be held on a much more regular basis than was the case with adults who didn't attend school. As we prayed about this matter, too, God was working. A new French-school director moved into the village, along with his large family. He turned out to be a Mundang who had had a number of years of experience teaching in northern Chad. Wadou was a Christian who remembered me from the time he was little. I occasionally preached and sold books in his Mundang village near Lere! Talk about God putting the pieces together! From the success that the Mundang children had who had gone through the Mundang literacy classes that we had set up among them years ago, he knew that the children could learn to read more quickly in the French-school in Mesken too, if they first knew how to read in their own language. So he quickly granted my request to begin literacy classes in his school. By this time (in the mid-1990s) we had already had printed four reading primers in the Bagirmi language. We just needed students for our literacy classes – and now we got them! So began several years of enjoyable daily contact with a number of Mesken children, some of whom became good readers in their language. One bright child even learned to read well by just his brother teaching him to read out of a book he had himself used in reading classes.

What about Blama Hassan, the chief? Well, he could certainly get an A for effort! He dropped out of my early literacy classes after a few weeks because of other work duties. But then, a couple of years later, he restarted – and had some 200 classes with me on a daily basis, starting usually at 5:30 or 6:00 in the morning, before he went off to his fields and orchard. Often I was invited to eat breakfast with him and our 30-minute class could be interrupted for that. But for not much else. He was very persistent! He did not learn to read well at all and we both felt badly about that. But he certainly wanted to. We suspected that he had dyslexia, a reading problem that he seemed to share with at least two of his children. There was no question at all of his intelligence.

Bright-colored folders started something important in Mesken village! Many people in the village have heard – some a number of times – stories from both the Old and the New Testaments. There are now books available in their language on not only the Bible (the Gospel of Mark is the latest that has been printed), but also books on their tribal history, folktales, and literacy books. Among the Mundang, book orders were in the thousands, but in the Bagirmi language they still number only in the dozens. But the Seed has been sown!

16
Yakub

Yakub was another person who was very important to people in the village. When people wanted a thatch-roof to stay on well, Yakub would be called upon to help. When a man intended to make a dugout canoe and he wanted the canoe to float without tipping to one side, he would want Yakub to size up his log and make the preliminary ax-marks to guide the canoe-makers in their ax-work. When the villagers needed a tripod over a newly-dug well so concrete casings could be lowered easily, they called on Yakub to rig it up. He could always be counted on to do things right and with seemingly little effort. He was a gifted man.

Yakub was not only a jack-of-all trades, but he was also one of the friendliest persons we had ever met. He would come to our house from time to time whenever he thought we needed a little fellowship. He would sit down on the woven palm mat offered him and would greet with an effusive display of hand motions accompanied by broad smiles and an occasional grunt. He would ask about our daughter and family living far away, how the weather was suiting us, how the termites were treating us – and we tried to answer him, but it wasn't always so easy.

One time my son and I were having a "discussion" with him about animals. At one point Yakub wasn't getting us to understand exactly what animal he had in mind. Suddenly he reached out to the damp soil around the mat (it had recently rained) and with several deft movements of his hand he drew a very good likeness of a baboon: face with deep-set eyes and all. No doubt any longer.

One of Yakub's daughters got married one day. When the festivities were over, I paid him a visit. He was sitting alone outside his house, looking a bit weary. He put his teapot on the fire and showed eagerness to have a quiet visit after the many distractions of the day. While we socialized, I noticed clouds coming up and I wondered if we weren't going to get an early start to our rainy season that year. Yakub didn't think so. He picked up a small berry from a large tree overhead and indicated by sounds of blowing and waving of hands that any wind coming along now would be just sound and fury without rain. "The seeds of this tree would have to get this large first and then the rains will come." This he "told" me by indicating with his fingers a bigger-sized berry and more whooshing sounds and vertical hand-movements. I no sooner got home that day than a tremendous four-inch rain came down, completely demolishing Yakub's weather forecasting. A couple of days later I sat down under the same tree with him and reminded him of his erroneous prediction and we had a good laugh together.

Another of Yakub's daughters came over one day with her baby. She was visiting her parents and had brought along her father to help her make her request. She thought her baby needed eye medicine. (Over the years Orpha treated many people in Mesken who had eye disease.) Yakub thought so, too, and looked sympathetically at his tiny granddaughter. The baby's eyes were not red or inflamed so Orpha and I judged that her crying was due to some other problem. The mother was definitely not convinced and was not at all happy that we would not put eye salve into her baby's eyes. Yakub looked like he was disappointed with us as they slowly walked away. I felt frustrated not being able to explain things better to my friend. And it was another time when we turned somebody down. That was something the Bagirmi didn't appreciate at all and it hurt us to treat Yakub like that.

The next day Yakub sought me out. As soon as he saw me in the village, he came over to me with a big smile. His daughter's baby had had a good night's sleep and woke up feeling fine. I was relieved! And I thought – wasn't that just like Yakub to want to put us at ease at his first opportunity? He knew we felt badly that we had to deny the medicine to the baby and he wanted to now tell me that we were right and they were wrong.

Lacking the ability to hear and speak never seemed to interfere much with Yakub's enjoyment of life and his ablility to cope with things. We will always remember him as a model of intelligence, good humor and an understanding heart.

17
"Be Prepared!"

We saw a lot of Al Haj, the village amulet-maker, over the years in Mesken. In our first couple of years there he was my faithful language teacher. But even long after the language classes ended, he would spend a lot of time at our place. Often this small, wiry man, in his late sixties and early seventies, needed help in repairing something – a broken canoe paddle, a house door, his wristwatch band, a mouse-trap ... One would never know what would be in his hands when he came walking towards our place!

One day he came by to greet us, all decked out in his going-to-market finery which included a clean white gown and a long 18-inch knife in plain view, giving the message to all would-be attackers: "Don't try messing with me!" That day he asked us, "Have you seen my corn field lately?" Then he related in detail the progress of his harvest labors. One could tell he was proud of his field – one of the largest in the village. He always worked hard. He wanted to make sure that he and his wife wouldn't go hungry.

Another day Al Haj and I were out on the highway, waiting for a vehicle to take us to N'Djamena. My car had broken down and couldn't take us there. Al Haj looked at me while we waited and asked, "Where's your knife?" I said I didn't have one. "Oh, you must have one hidden on you somewhere," he said. "No," I said while looking at his ever-present knife, "I have a better Protector with me; He is like a shepherd always taking care of me." Al Haj didn't know what to make of that. He seemed to think I was very careless not to carry a knife.

I usually enjoyed my times with Al Haj as we worked together on things or simply chatted. He loved to talk and I would learn things. He was generally congenial and friendly. And he wasn't bashful to ask for things. Sometimes he wanted to borrow our wheelbarrow to haul home his grain or to haul mud for house-building, other times it would be a spade or a hammer or some nails. Or maybe he would come just to lie down on a mat in our yard and take a snooze! Or to simply sit quietly and enjoy the peace that he sensed around our place. One of those times he told me that we must have some "dawa" around. "Dawa" is a word referring to any kind of medicine or magical protective power. Certainly we had a protective Power – but not the "dawa" in his world of dealing with things!

One day Al Haj came over with something different. A chunk of rhinoceros horn! He told me how he had long ago come into possession of this "valuable" object and he said it had served him well: he had made and sold many charms from it. When I saw him come that day, I thought I would read the story of Joseph to him. When I saw what he was about to do, I still went ahead and started reading. As he sat on the mat, he began scraping with his knife on that horn and gathering the filings for making new amulets. I suppose I could have chased him away – thus showing my disappoval of his trade in a rather forceful way he wouldn't have forgotten. But I would probably have lost a seeker of God in the process. As it was, he quietly sat while he worked and listened to a story in the Bible about a man whom God had so wonderfully protected during his life. And many times since that day he has listened to God's Word being read.

Once Al Haj came over and told me about the work he'd done that morning. He had just killed 41 chickens – a sacrifice for getting Allah to guard the village fields from plant pests. That's what he told me. Was the sacrifice really made to Allah or to the spirits? I believe that neither he nor many others really made much distinction between the two. They seemed to treat Allah very much like the spirits they were always trying to manipulate!

Al Haj knew a lot about taking precautions. He was always so busy getting himself and the village ready for any contingency. His motto could certainly have been, "Be prepared!". Knives, amulets, making sacrifices, planting large fields – they all helped, he felt. But I wondered at times if he didn't sense a need for more than all these to get him through the uncertainties ahead.

I believe he knew that there was some kind of "dawa" connected to the Scriptures. During a recent trip that we made back to the village after having been gone for over three years, Al Haj came over to our place one day while my son and I were working on our car. He asked me if I had something I could read to him. I certainly did, and he sat and listened attentively for over half an hour as I read from the Bible.

The man who once left our yard in a huff because I had told him more than he wanted to hear that day about Jesus and the salvation He was offering him, will he someday remember that conversation and the many other things he has heard from Scripture readings over the years and then fully realize that his attempts to always be prepared have really been very flimsy and futile? We still pray for this man who so captured my heart, even though he could be very cantakerous and negative at times. And yes, even though he was and still is, as far as we know, the village witchdoctor and amulet-maker!

18
124,000 Prophets!

One morning in the middle of the rainy season, I walked down to the middle of the village. Groups of men were sitting on mats here and there. Everyone was intent on his prayer beads, everyone was furiously reciting something. At intervals there were shouts and someone was recording something after each shout. What was going on? I wondered. I sat down on one mat, after a while I sat down on another. There were no greetings, each man worked grimly at his task.

I asked Kusu the next morning about this. "Oh," he said, "we were reciting the first 'sura' (chapter) of the Quran." He went on to explain the ritual they had been performing: Each person is to recite as many times as he can the first chapter of the Quran (which includes the words: "You alone we worship, and to you alone we turn for help."). Each time he finishes reciting this sura, he moves another bead along the string, thus keeping track of the number of times he has recited. At intervals, someone in each group adds up how many times that sura has been recited by his group and shouts the number out to someone who is keeping track of the collective number of times it has been recited. The goal is to repeat this sura 124,000 times. If a village cannot finish in one day, they can continue the next day. But the goal must be reached before they can petition Allah to bring them the aid they want – at this particular time they badly needed more rain for the crops. About 100 men were available in Mesken village for this recital, Kusu told me. Women could not participate in this public event – although they could count their beads in their homes. It was unclear to me whether or not their recitals would in this case be accepted by men as having any value – but probably not.

This ritual is based on the number of prophets that exist according to Islamic belief. They number 124,000, although only

25 – some say 28 – are mentioned by name in the Quran. Six have particular importance and are given special names. These prophets are Adam, Noah, Abraham, Moses, Jesus and Muhammad. So when there are really important reasons for getting Allah to move, they must repeat this sura 124,000 times in order to bring all the prophets into the act somehow. Kusu said that they may even recite the first sura more than 124,000 times for extra merit!

We next got into a long discussion on how our faiths differ. We had been translating God as "Heavenly Father" in the Bible whenever the text demanded it. I asked Kusu about this because I knew that he did not like when God was called Heavenly Father. Again he reminded me that we can only call God our master, because we are his slaves. I asked him that when our faiths differ so strikingly and I am coming with all kinds of things that Muslims don't believe in: "Why do you people let us live in your village? Why don't you chase us out?" His answer: "Because you are among the People of the Book. We are really following one religion; we all believe in one God." "But we believe differently, we don't follow the same beliefs," I said. Well, he thought that we could each follow our religion "side by side." And besides, "you people are good to us and we could never chase you out."

Prayer group outside of mosque

I think our discussion went along those lines because we were each following the mentality of our respective cultures. In the West, logical consistency, honesty, reliability and moral courage are top virtues. We tend to despise people who lie, steal and act cowardly and inconsistently. The Oriental mind sees things differently – and the Africans I've known certainly have the Oriental mind – hospitality, patience and courtesy, along with a group spirit, are the top virtues. Kusu was not being consistent and maybe not even completely truthful – but he was showing courtesy and hospitality. He was being patient with me. It wasn't the first nor the last time that our discussions wouldn't get anywhere! As far as showing Islam to be illogical and Christianity logical, I never really wanted to go far down that road and tried to stay out of arguments. I kept trying to recite what the Bible says and let it go at that, trusting God's Holy Spirit to bring enlightenment to Kusu.

Not long after the above discussion I read that the New Testament was published in Kyrgyzstan (one of the former Soviet republics and largely Muslim) in 1992, about the same time as a version of the Quran in their language came to them. "Many have compared the two and are favorably impressed with the Bible message," the book said. That was encouraging to me. Turkish armies brought Islam into their country in the 17th century, but the Bible, when it finally reached them, "favorably impressed" them! The Bible speaks about the God who can be reached without having to appeal to 124,000 prophets first! This is very appealing to people living in desperate situations.

19
Work and Play in a Chadian Village

Already the western bank of the Chari was coming alive. The eastern sky was turning to a more vibrant color and one could now see and not just hear the men bailing water out of the canoes. The fishermen were out getting their dugouts and fishing nets in order. Soon they would be out in the river, silhouetted against the first golden rays of a rapidly rising sun. Soon one would see them laying their nets. There would be more noise later as women came to the river to wash their cooking utensils. But for now, total silence except for the splashing of water by the bailers, and the occasional screech of the river birds.

Later, too, would come the men and boys with their canoe-repairing equipment: old bicycle tires, awls and axes, pieces of wood and string, bundles of tough river grass. Old rotten wood would be replaced by newer pieces on the canoe bottoms and sides. Holes would be patched so the water bailing could be less. Old rubber and tough grass would be stuffed as caulking between the old wood and the new and the pieces of wood would be lashed together by nylon string. The kind of work that had been done for centuries – long before the bicycle tires had come along. Skills that had been handed down from father to son.

When the sun was high, women would come to the river with their laundry – and a little later, the men with theirs, after other work had been done. Here there was no shame for men to wash clothes – only their own, of course. Old men would sometimes come and sit on the warm sand of the river-bank to try and catch some cooling breeze at mid-day. Pick-up trucks would descend to the river at any hour and pick up loads of wood to take to N'Djamena to sell – for making charcoal or for holding up house roofs. Trees were rapidly disappearing on our side of the river. The wood now would often come by canoe from across the river. When we first came, monkeys would sometimes sit in the large trees. Now they were becoming scarcer as the trees became scarcer.

Men and women would walk past our house and often greet as they went to their fields in early morning: the men to their corn fields or huge tomato plots; the women to their fields of peanuts, gumbo and other plants they use for making their sauces to serve with the corn or for drinks to sell at the markets. Or some would stay home to cook food to carry out to the men in the fields, enabling them to work longer. At harvest time in the fall, women and children would carry the crops home – on their heads, of course. As soon as the heavy rains were over, the men would carry out their tomato plants they had started in small plots by the big river and transplant them in the huge plots by the small river – or sometimes by the big one. Along these two rivers, the Chari and the Loumia, were the diesel irrigation pumps which pumped water into the maze of ditches that fed water to the tomato plants. Women and children would be recruited to help pick and carry home the tomato harvest, but the irrigating and cultivating work would be done only by men and boys. Pick-up trucks would drive out to the more accessible tomato fields and would often start out in the wee hours of the morning for N'Djamena with their loads that would be sold in the big markets there. Tomatoes were the cash commodity in our village by the time we got there, replacing cotton and fish of the past. Cotton had been rapidly depleting the soil and the fish were becoming more scarce. Aid organizations had come to the rescue to supply pumps and irrigation pipes for the tomato industry. Mesken owes much to such organizations. For some who didn't like working in the tomato fields, cutting trees and hauling wood to city markets was a more interesting and profitable venture – which explains why that part of Chad is being rapidly denuded of trees. Who replants the trees? Guess!

Each Saturday a big market a couple miles away would empty the village of all but the old and infirm and the small children who would stay with them. If there was extra corn, that would be taken and sold there. Or gumbo. Or a sheep or goat or two would be taken. Or food and drink specialities for the hungry and thirsty at the all-day market. Many women knew how to make a refreshing drink that resembled cranberry juice. Others made a doughnut-like pastry called makala. Market-day was a special time for most everybody as people from a number of small villages converged there as well as wholesale buyers and sellers from N'Djamena.

Late afternoons people would stream home from the market. Arab women with their bright yellow, red and orange wrap-arounds and headscarfs would talk the loudest and look the flashiest. They lived in villages across the Chari. Bagirmi women, dressed in more subdued tones, also had lots to say as they shared the news they heard that day. Often we would see the small children run to meet their mothers on the path – and would often be given candy purchased at the market. The fathers would come home in the pick-ups which charged five or ten cents for the ride.

The children in Mesken could not be entertained by toys bought in the market. Except for the occasional ball, there were no toys there! So they did what most children in Africa still do – make their own toys and invent their own games. The little girls and boys often made their own "pretend" markets out of mud and sticks. The "confections" they "sold" would look a lot like our mud pies and cookies of a long time ago. I'm sure the leaves and grass they "sold" tasted just as good, too. Sometimes

Boys making toy truck

I would stop and pretend I wanted to buy – and they would shyly giggle.

The bigger girls often played hopscotch and jacks – like we did 60 years ago! What they played with, though, showed imagination.

A favorite pastime of boys was building cars and trucks out of pieces of corn stalks. Thorn needles held the pieces together and pieces of gourd would be cut in disks and used for wheels. These vehicles were often very intricately made – with doors and hoods that opened and with "engines" inside and wheels that could be turned to the right or left. Their ingenuity amazed me! Small boys often pushed hoops around. The better ones were old bicycle rims. Or they would pull each other around using old plastic fuel containers cut in half. Or they would kick around a small ball made of strings or rags wound around. Bigger boys used real soccer balls, though, when they played that popular game.

Our son, David, introduced a game that became very popular among the young men. As children in America, we got a large Chinese Checkers game with a sturdy Masonite board on Christmas Eve, 1941. I brought it out to Africa many years ago and we played the game many times in our home. But the board still had some life left in it and we managed to keep the marbles, too. So David took it down to the village one day and showed the young men how to play. It was an immediate hit! Some of them liked to cheat at it, though, and every once in a while, one of the two guys who had the most authority among them got disgusted and bounced the board, upsetting the marbles. And they'd start all over.

Traditional games, too, were played, using berries and pieces of charcoal for markers. And kids made snares and traps with which to catch birds, providing tasty snacks! A common kind was to lay a string fastened to small round chunks of clay under the surface of the sandy soil. On the surface would be sprinkled some seeds or corn which the birds liked and those birds would scratch around and peck away while their feet would get tangled in the string under the surface. And little hands would quickly grab the hapless victims. Tricky, I thought!

20
Hawa Leaves Us

When we arrived in Mesken, Hawa was a little girl of six. I don't remember her from then, but I suppose she was one of the many children who were constantly running in and out of Grandpa Ada's compound. Over the years, his living space would become smaller as each of his five sons would take a wife and move next door to the family patriarch.

One day one of Ada's daughters-in-law came over with a tiny scrawny baby – little more than skin stretched over a skeleton. It was clearly dying. It was also clear that the mother wanted very much to keep this child. Orpha diagnosed the problem correctly and started feeding him milk mixed with sugar and salt. We were amazed that this tiny mite with his over-sized head could raise himself up and eagerly start drinking the way he did. Just a tiny bit at first, but then more and more. After some days the child had improved to the extent that the mother stopped coming to our door. She was very grateful and when Hamat grew older, she told him about the kind lady who had saved his life. This child was a young brother of Hawa.

I would often visit Ada. I was especially interested in him since the time I dreamed of him and his wife becoming radiant Christians. I badly wanted the dream to become reality because they seemed so happy in the dream. He did indeed become more and more interested in what the Word of God had to say and would often ask me to read while sitting with other men in the village. When he became too feeble to do so any longer, I would come to his house. I was always welcomed by either his wife or any one of his daughters-in-law who was around. And he himself always welcomed me with a hearty handshake and a large smile.

Then Ada became deathly sick. I would go and read a bit and pray for him as he lay very still in his tiny sleeping hut. He could hardly speak and it became more difficult for him to breathe. After some days, I suggested to his family that we move him to a small hospital up the highway a little ways. At first they resisted the idea, preferring to have him die at home. But then they relented and one morning we set off with our old station wagon crammed with Ada and as many family members as could possibly get in – along with sleeping mats and pots and pans. Ada remained at the primitive-looking hospital with its mud-walled buildings a number of days. God was answering our prayers as my old friend steadily improved. When he had gained enough strength to return home, I again moved Ada and household back to Mesken. The family was very grateful to me and, I think, also to God.

One time when I was over at Ada's house, I had a camera with me. Hawa, now in her mid-teens, was also there, along with a number of small cousins. I thought it would be nice to get a couple pictures and when I suggested that to Hawa, she quickly picked up a large club that is used for pounding corn

Hawa and retarded friend

and posed with that as though she were pounding corn in the mortar in front of her. Before I took the second picture, she pulled an older girl towards her – a girl that had some mental problem and thus the butt of pranks – and she put her arm around this girl while I snapped the picture. That was Hawa, thinking about others! She was a popular girl in the village and it was easy to see why. The Mundang French-school director and his family lived right next to Hawa's father's compound and the director's oldest daughter was about the age of Hawa and a committed Christian. Hawa and Seline became good friends.

Hawa became deathly sick one time while we were in N'Djamena for several days. When we returned, Hawa was gone! She had "stepped over the threshold" as they say in Bagirmi. She was being treated at a nearby dispensary for a severe case of malaria and she seemed to be improving. Then for some inexplicable reason Hawa's family was persuaded to have her taken off the "white man's treatment" and she was put into the hands of some traditional medicine man. (Was it Al Haj? I never did find out.) Hawa died shortly after.

The villagers and especially the young people were shocked and very upset. Their neighbor, the Christian school director, told us afterwards that the death was completely "needless" as she may well have stayed alive if she had continued being treated in the correct way. There were days of mourning following her burial. I sat under the large trees with the men outside Hawa's family compound. One day I started reading Psalm 34 in the Bagirmi language to several men sitting next to me on a mat. Talking among the other men soon slowed and finally stopped by the time I reached the end: "God comes to the aid of those who follow him. Those who run to hide themselves in God will not know God's judgment." It was a sober moment. Talk about the end times followed. Muslims believe that the end of the world with its Judgment Day will come 10,000 years after the world was created. And those 10,000 years have just about run their course, they say. Many Muslims believe that Jesus will descend and destroy an evil figure who will work especially hard in the Last Days to lead people away from Allah (by doing spectacular miracles, using sensual music, etc.) and then

Muhammad will be raised to life and Jesus and Muhammad will team up and win the entire world to Islam. We didn't talk about all this then, but questions arose about Y2-K and will the year 2000 usher in Judgment Day and the end of the world as it now stands? As to just when the world would end, I couldn't tell them, but I pointed out some of the signs that would signal the coming of Jesus and the Day of Judgment according to the Bible.

Was the death of Hawa without consequence? True, it was "needless", according to the way we see things. But did God have a higher purpose in this strange death? I cannot doubt but that God will someday turn this unforgettable event into something good! We believe it is possible that Hawa died as a Christian although we never heard that she turned to Christ. But then, there are many things that Muslims and ex-Muslims do not tell the white man, nor even each other, sometimes for good reason. Sixteen-year-old Hawa was to have been married to a Muslim two or three weeks after she died. Would it have been likely that her new faith in Christ – assuming that she did become a believer – would have survived this union to a Muslim?

Hawa's mother came over a couple weeks after Hawa's death. It was clear that she had been grieving much over the death of her daughter who had been such a helpful companion to her. Now she was left only with Hamat who was now a sturdy seven or eight-year-old, a smaller girl, and a married daughter. Very likely Hawa's mother had lost several children in between those who were living. What will come of Hamat, the "miracle baby?" As to Ada, when we left Chad in 1999, we wondered how it would go with him. We dreaded ever to hear the news that he passed away because we weren't sure of his spiritual state. Then one day a couple years ago we heard he had died. But neither Orpha nor I felt anything other than peace when we heard of Ada's death. Later we heard more. His wife would not allow the usual mourning sacrifices and other traditional things following his death and this was scandalous to the village. Does her conduct indicate that she and her husband left the old ways and had become new creatures in Christ? Will we see them again? May God grant that it be so!

21
Battles and Struggles

We heard the loud and weird whizzing sound drawing closer to Mesken village. We saw the sky darken as thousands of flying insects swept overhead. Would they continue on or would they descend and strip the corn fields, the mango trees and the rice paddies of their green parts? The villagers were determined to keep them from landing. Their method was to beat as many pots and pans as they could muster and make as much noise as they possibly could. Fighting a battle... of locust invasion, a dreaded prospect every few years. This time the villagers won – sometimes they don't.

Another day David had just left our house to go on a book-selling trip. I entered our small 4 by 6 foot storehouse to get kerosene for filling on our refrigerator. I reached down to pick up a fuel jerrycan – and was surprised by the presence of a large cobra lurking just behind it. I yelled for Orpha to come and bring our long-handled spade with the squared-off edge we kept handy for such emergencies. Between the two of us we managed to pin the cobra to the floor with the spade and beat it to death with another implement – a shovel or whatever, I have now forgotten. But it took about 45 minutes of work. Cobras when cornered are very aggressive and it got away from us once or twice. Its seven-foot length indicated it was a female – they are larger than the males. Fighting another battle... of cobra invasion. Chadians tend to leave a dangerous snake like that alone, but we decided that it was necessary to rid the storehouse of it or we wouldn't dare to enter it another time.

There were many more ordinary struggles of everyday living in our village. Things wear out and break down. People with extremely low incomes welcome the services of itinerant menders of things. There were those who would come around to replace rusted-out bottoms of pots and kettles with pieces of cast-away tin cans. Others repaired old sieves and teapots, and old radios and cassette-players for the more "wealthy". It was interesting to see how these itinerant craftsmen worked. A roving blacksmith was the center of attention one day in the village. I asked him about his various tools. All – the tongs, bellows, awl, hammer, scissors – seemed to be homemade, and with these he made and repaired things on the spot. Another time two men stayed several days and got the radios and players around the village in working order again – for a little while. How they managed to do so was a mystery to me as I observed parts and pieces spread all over the ground around them.

Having enough water for our needs seemed to always be a struggle for us. We discovered early on that the Bagirmi people scorned working as common laborers for others – maybe a holdover trait from the days when they were the conquerors of other tribes and had slaves to do much of their own manual work. So we couldn't get anyone to regularly carry water for us. At first we had to use our car to haul water from other villages and later, when our village got its own well, David carried water in containers with our wheelbarrow. In the rainy season, we had rain gutters that would lead water into the steel drums we placed under them. During the rainy season when water was abundant, neighbors would come over and get water from us. And after

Itinerant radio repairmen

77

several years, we saw several metal roofs go up and our rain gutters were imitated. Getting enough good water was a battle we shared with the villagers. River water was becoming more and more contaminated.

There was a time towards the end of our stay in the village when there seemed to be more spiritual battles than usual. There was apathy and indifference on the part of villagers towards the message from the Bible we sought to bring them. Even Kusu became quite argumentative and negative as we worked together. He began complaining about the different writers of the Gospels. Why, their stories didn't even always jibe! he noticed. He began grousing about the original text of the Bible (which the Quran concedes is a helpful guide but not the final word) having been corrupted since the time of Muhammad. He had never done that before. It was the time when the American president was rapidly losing the respect of the villagers and Kusu himself was affected by the president's immoral behavior. He began to lose some respect for us and the Christian Bible as a result.

Experiencing battles and struggles of one kind or another is not fun – and yet, God uses them for character-building and to make us more dependent on Him. In our last year in the village we had more sickness than we ever had and it was a constant battle just to keep going. But at that time books again "rescued" me. A couple of Charles Colson's books, *Loving God* and *Against the Night*, were very helpful. I was reminded again that God never demands more from us than He is prepared to give.

22
Subversive Activity

It was tomato-picking time in our village and I came upon Dadi, patching one of his tomato crates. It would soon be filled and hauled, along with many others, to the N'Djamena markets. He showed me the design of a chameleon on all four sides of each crate, somewhat crudely sketched on with a marking pen. For one living in an area where adults don't know how to read or write, this is a neat expedient for identifying one's belongings. Dadi and others in the village would know those crates belonged to him when the crates would be returned empty from the markets. I wondered why he used that particular logo. Dadi smilingly explained to me that the chameleon was a symbol of himself: "Little by little, I move forward."

Is the chameleon a symbol we would choose for a logo for identifying ourselves? Maybe a bear or eagle or even a rooster. But a chameleon? Probably not! There are too many negative things to say about these creatures. They're sneaky, changing color all the time to suit the environment. They move too slowly, becoming easy prey for predators. And they're downright ugly! But maybe even a lowly chameleon can teach us a thing or two.

The chameleon does not appear too threatening to anybody or anything as he slowly and stealthily moves along, his protruding revolving eyes ever on the alert. In a way, he is somewhat subversive. You are apt to think he'll get nowhere the way he moves. He's no threat, so let him be. But watch him. With lightning swiftness his long tongue grabs the unsuspecting fly that he's been after.

Some day the Word of God that many of the Mesken villagers heard while we lived there is going to take effect. It, too, is in a sense subversive. It seems weak and incapable of accomplishing much, but we must never be fooled! It is very active and powerful beyond human comprehension. The villagers heard over and over the accounts of Joseph's and Abraham's lives in the Old Teatament and the simple parables and healing stories in the New Testament. To them they were wonderful stories. They listened and felt there would be no harm in doing so. Their defenses were down. But one day, the stories will grab them. All their religiosity will then seem futile and they will see themslves as the lowly tax collector or the prodigal son crying out for forgiveness from their Heavenly Father!

I believe Kusu will not easily forget those stories – and the many discussions they engendered. While working with him day after day for a period of over six years, God's Word was working quietly in Kusu's heart and mind. God's holiness and grace (both concepts totally lacking in Islam) baffled Kusu as they do all Muslims. The Bible's idea of God's holiness seemed too stringent; its idea of grace too easy! At times we would discuss assurance of salvation, that is, knowing that one is right with God. One day I was asking him about an Arab term that denotes a purgatory-like place after death. I asked him if all Muslims must suffer in this place. He replied that very rarely does a Muslim escape going there, but what will really happen is never known in this life. In other words, one doesn't know in advance of the Day of Judgment whether or not God is satisfied with one's record of good works. One's record determines whether or how long a Muslim would have to stay in this place of suffering and which level he would find himself in, there being several levels of severity of suffering. Again I had the chance to tell him that the believer in Christ Jesus has, according to the Bible, the certainty of entering directly into His presence after death. It was something he would have liked to believe, I felt, but he could not be a Muslim and believe it.

Often when somebody was about to travel somewhere, that person would put a coin in Kusu's hands and ask him to recite something from the Quran – a prayer, I assume, for protection. Or they would sit on his mat and ask him to help them recite the Quran for themselves or to explain something on Islam. Kusu was highly respected for his devotion and knowledge. I have often prayed that he would some day become a believer in Christ and be the one in the village to explain God's Word to people.

Sometimes I had the feeling that he was close to the Kingdom of God; I wrote once in my journal after a long talk with him about the work of Jesus that he "seems to want to hear my arguments from the Scriptures as though he's not really sure of Islam and wants to know more what I believe." He never said anything derogatory about Jesus and he generally respected the Bible. He wanted the Bible to be translated into his language. We could say the same for most of the people in the village. Aren't these signs that the subversive activity of God's Word was silently wearing down resistance and preparing for the day when they would be totally "grabbed" by its truth?

Everyone helps carry tomatoes

Final Words

In the fall of 1999, we abruptly left Africa! A break in the concrete floor of a mission guest-house kitchen in N'Djamena brought about a dramatic change in our lives. Orpha was preparing the evening meal and suddenly she tripped and fell. What we had first thought was merely a bad sprain turned out to be a fractured hip bone! For a week Orpha lay still on a guest-house bed until arrangements were completed for an evacuation on the next available Air France flight. 24 hours after we boarded that flight we found ourselves at the Fergus Falls, Minnesota, airport. A couple days later was the hip surgery. And three months later a couple surgeries for me – for cancer I didn't know I had.

When we left N'Djamena we didn't think we would ever return to Chad. And yet, three and a half years later, we actually did! Our oldest son, Jonathan, had informed us that there would be a wedding in the spring of 2003 and would I perform the ceremony? He described in a letter the girl that God had chosen for him. Her name was Zamzam, a convert from Islam. We found our old traveling gear that we thought we had stowed away for good and were off for a three-month trip to Chad. The wedding was a very special one with people of many different backgrounds present. There were southern Chadian Christians and northern Chadian Arabs – representatives from both sides of Zamzam's family. And missionaries from various missions. And a couple of Mundang friends we knew from long ago. And the Mesken chief, accompanied by his brother.

We spent most of the three months with our son David and the villagers in Mesken. They were astounded to see us back! I picked up with Kusu where we left off several years earlier and we did some badly needed checking of translation work. I won't forget the day I read Acts 2 and 3 for checking. One of those sitting around listening came closer and stood directly behind me for maybe 40 minutes drinking in the words! The villagers were more cordial to us than ever and I found many chances to visit and pray with the sick in their homes. And on those long tropical evenings under the stars it was wonderful to have those conversations with David again.

Our newest grandchild, Esther, was born to Jonathan and Zamzam at 3:A.M. on January 11, 2004 (8 P.M. on January, 10 CST) after a strenuous night of chasing down the doctor in N'Djamena and trying to keep the mid-wife awake. The doctor was nervous as he performed the unexpected and necessary C-section surgery, but was calmed after Jonathan assured him that many were praying for him and the birth.

We long to visit again, under Chadian skies, the rest of our family. Will that be, and if so, when? We leave that to our faithful Heavenly Father Who has delightfully surprised us so many times.

Celebrating our 40th in a N'Djamena restaurant
(10 years ago – last time we were all together)